AF568062

THE POWER OF SAYING NO!

Ashutosh Garg worked in the corporate sector for twenty-five years before becoming an entrepreneur and founding the extremely popular Guardian Pharmacy chain in 2003. He also served as director of GAVI, the Vaccine Alliance (headquartered in Geneva), for eight years and has been a member of several other prestigious boards. Recognized as a Global Leader for Tomorrow by the World Economic Forum in 1995, he is an active member of the Young Presidents' Organization, the world's largest leadership community, and a charter member of TiE or The Indus Entrepreneurs.

He launched the popular global podcast 'The Brand Called You' (www.tbcy.in) in 2019 and has written ten highly acclaimed books, including the bestseller *7 Chakras of Management*, and can frequently be seen on national television discussing current affairs. A keen golfer, he also plays the Indian flute and enjoys reading.

THE POWER OF SAYING NO!

Why Really Successful People Say NO to Almost Everything

Ashutosh Garg

RUPA

Published by
Rupa Publications India Pvt. Ltd 2025
161-B/4, Gulmohar House,
Yusuf Sarai Community Centre,
New Delhi 110049

Sales centres:
Bengaluru Chennai
Hyderabad Kolkata Mumbai

P-ISBN: 978-93-7003-807-3
E-ISBN: 978-93-7003-540-9

First impression 2025

10 9 8 7 6 5 4 3 2 1

Printed in India

Dedicated to

Our granddaughter
Vaani

My wife
Vera

Our sons
Varun and Ashwin

Our daughters-in-law
Sakshi and Jody

My mother
Sudha Garg

My father
Brig ML Garg, AVSM, Kirti Chakra

Contents

Introduction

Saying no is a fundamental aspect of human interaction, conveying boundaries, autonomy and personal ethics. Despite its brevity, a 'no' carries significant emotional and psychological weight. The ability to say it to oneself is the beginning of true freedom.

Saying no is also an expression of self-control. I will discuss this in much greater detail in this book. The Bhagavad Gita states, 'One who has control over the mind and senses is serene amidst pleasures and pains, honour and dishonour.'[1]

▪

Many years back while travelling with some very senior colleagues in China, I asked the chairman of a major US company—who had businesses here and in India—what he felt was the difference between Indian managers (or entrepreneurs) and Chinese.

His answer amazed me. I have not only not forgotten his answer but shared it many times in conversations and at conferences. He said:

'It is very difficult to get a Chinese manager or entrepreneur to say yes and it is very difficult to get an Indian manager or entrepreneur to say no!'

---

[1]Bhagavad Gita, 6.7.

I have often thought of these wise words and over the years of working as a professional manager and an entrepreneur, I have realized that these words ring true, whether we like it or not.

We find it very difficult to say no.

Over the years, I have realized that it is not just Indians but virtually everyone faces the challenge of saying no. Each person's reason for not being able to say no could be different and everyone has a way to rationalize for their response.

Yet, how many of us wish we had the ability or the courage to say no when confronted with the option rather than getting stuck in an awkward situation or doing a shoddy piece of work—something we would not be proud of.

All because we did not say no at the right time.

▪

The concept of saying no and the power of setting boundaries are not explicitly addressed in traditional Hindu scriptures in the way modern psychology or self-help literature discusses them.

However, several scriptures and teachings from the Vedas, Upanishads, Ramayana, Mahabharata, Bhagavad Gita, as well as insights from Chanakya, Osho and Jiddu Krishnamurti provide wisdom on discernment, self-control, and the importance of maintaining one's integrity and inner peace.

Hindu scriptures emphasize the importance of discernment and the ability to say no in various contexts, highlighting the virtue of saying no as a form of self-control, righteousness and wisdom. I have picked up three narratives from the Gita, the Katha Upanishad and the Shanti Parva of the Mahabharata to illustrate my thoughts.

The Bhagavad Gita (Chapter 2, Verse 47) states:

कर्मण्येवाधिकारस्ते मा फलेषु कदाचन।
मा कर्मफलहेतुर्भूर्मा ते सङ्गोऽस्त्वकर्मणि।।[2]

The literal translation of this verse, which is a part of most of our everyday life, is that we have a right to perform our prescribed duties, but we are not entitled to expect the fruits of our actions. We must never consider ourselves the cause of the results of our activities, nor be attached to inaction.

This verse teaches us the importance of performing one's duty without attachment to the results. It implicitly advises saying no to desires and attachments that may lead one away from righteous action. Saying no here is about rejecting the temptation of seeking personal gains or rewards from one's actions and focusing instead on duty and righteousness. It promotes the idea of detachment, where saying 'no' leads to spiritual growth and inner peace.

The Katha Upanishad (Verse 1.2.24) states:

नाविरतो दुश्चरितान्नाशान्तो नासमाहितः ।
नाशान्तमानसो वापि प्रज्ञानेनैनमाप्नुयात् ॥२४॥[3]

The verse translates to: 'This is the path of the wise, not of the ignorant. The wise, having realized the supreme reality, do not seek transient pleasure.'

In this part, Yama, the lord of death, is instructing Nachiketa on the wisdom of rejecting temporary pleasures for the pursuit of higher knowledge and self-realization.

---

[2]Bhagavad Gita, 2.47.

[3]Katha Upanishad, 1.2.24.

This is a direct encouragement to say no to distractions and temptations that deviate one from the spiritual path. The verse teaches that the ability to say no is a form of spiritual discernment, allowing one to prioritize the pursuit of eternal truth over fleeting pleasures.

A verse from the Shanti Parva of the Mahabharata (Book 12, Chapter 19) states:

धर्मो हि हतो हन्ति, धर्मो रक्षति रक्षितः।
तस्माद्धर्मो न हन्तव्यः, मा नो धर्मो हतोऽवधीत्॥[4]

This passage underscores the importance of upholding *dharma* (righteousness or duty). In this context, saying no is about rejecting actions that violate dharma. It implies a rejection of unethical or unrighteous behaviour, emphasizing that one must say no to actions or decisions that could lead to the destruction of moral order. The power of saying no here is associated with protecting oneself and society from the consequences of *adharma* (unrighteousness).

Hindu scriptures collectively emphasize the power of saying no as a form of self-control, wisdom and adherence to dharma.

Whether it is resisting temptations, avoiding attachment to the fruits of actions, or rejecting actions contrary to one's moral duties, the ability to say no is portrayed as a crucial aspect of spiritual and ethical life. The scriptures encourage discernment and the courage to reject what is not beneficial to one's spiritual progress and the welfare of society.

▪

[4]Mahabharata, Shanti Parva, Book 12, Chapter 19.

I have always been an ardent follower of the teachings of Chanakya, the ancient Indian philosopher, economist and statesman, who is often regarded as one of the most influential figures in shaping the political and administrative framework of India. His seminal work, the *Arthashastra* (I have a copy of this book next to my bedside and read one page almost every day), provides detailed advice on statecraft, governance and diplomacy, offering timeless wisdom applicable to various aspects of life.

For Chanakya, the act of saying no is deeply rooted in discernment. He believed that an individual must always assess the situation carefully before making decisions. According to him, not every opportunity or request is beneficial, and agreeing to everything may lead to negative outcomes. One of the key teachings from the *Arthashastra* is that a wise leader or individual must weigh the pros and cons of a situation before committing to it.

The ability to say no is an essential skill in maintaining one's integrity and protecting one's interests.

In Chanakya's view, saying yes when one shouldn't can lead to exploitation or harm. People who lack the courage to refuse can be easily manipulated. Thus, he advised leaders to be cautious in their dealings, ensuring that they only agree to things that align with their objectives and values. This applies not just in the realm of politics but in personal relationships as well. Chanakya's emphasis on discernment highlights the importance of self-awareness and boundary-setting.

▪

In a world driven by productivity, social obligations and constant connectivity, the ability to say no has become an increasingly rare skill. While many pride themselves on being accommodating and generous with their time, energy and resources, this tendency can often lead to burnout, resentment and a diluted sense of purpose.

Learning to say no, especially in a culture that glorifies being busy and selfless, is essential for maintaining one's mental health, happiness, and personal fulfilment. The importance of saying no goes beyond the mere refusal of an invitation or task.

It is about creating space for what truly matters in life. It allows individuals to prioritize their own needs, set boundaries, and foster a life that aligns with their values. Despite its importance, many struggle with saying no, feeling guilt, fear of disappointing others, or a sense of obligation to constantly please.

However, mastering the art of saying no can empower individuals to take control of their lives, reduce stress, and focus on their true passions. Like most people, I too have struggled to say no innumerable times and regretted not having done so later.

The art of saying no is not about rejecting others, but about embracing one's own needs and priorities. It is a powerful tool for self-care, enabling individuals to lead more balanced and fulfilling lives.

By overcoming the common fears and misconceptions on this matter, and learning to communicate boundaries effectively, we can reclaim our time, energy, and happiness. Ultimately, the ability to say no is an act of self-respect and empowerment that can transform one's personal and professional life.

Agreeing to disagree is an empowering act that embraces

the value of no without seeking conflict or validation from others. It is a reminder that it is okay to hold different views and that relationships do not always require complete alignment. The power of saying no comes into play when you stand firm in your beliefs, values or boundaries while respectfully allowing others to maintain their own.

By agreeing to disagree, we acknowledge that consensus is not always achievable or even necessary. This acceptance brings clarity, enabling us to communicate that our perspective matters without needing to prove others wrong. It is a conscious decision to honour differences while protecting our own mental, emotional, or physical energy.

The power of no is further amplified in this context because it allows you to maintain integrity and avoid unnecessary stress. Saying no does not have to come with tension. It can simply be a clear boundary in understanding that not all situations require compromise. Agreeing to disagree is a mature, empowering stance, encouraging growth in relationships by fostering respect for each person's individual path.

▪

Dalai Lama also speaks about the importance of balancing compassion for others with compassion for oneself. In his book *The Art of Happiness*, he writes, 'Our prime purpose in this life is to help others. And if you can't help them, at least don't hurt them.' This teaching reminds us to consider our own limitations when someone reaches out for help. Saying no when we are overextended or emotionally drained is a way of honouring both ourselves and those we care about, ensuring that we can continue to give from a place of abundance rather than depletion.

In the words of Warren Buffett, 'The difference between successful people and really successful people is that really successful people say no to almost everything.'

▪

Steve Jobs emphasized the importance of saying no as a critical element of focus and success. One of his most famous quotes on the subject is: 'Focusing is about saying no. You have to say no to 1,000 things to make sure you don't get on the wrong track or try to do too much.'

Jobs believed that innovation and excellence require discipline and prioritization. He argued that saying 'no is not just about rejecting bad ideas but also about turning down many good ones to concentrate on what truly matters.'

In another instance, he said: 'People think focus means saying yes to the thing you've got to focus on. But that's not what it means at all. It means saying no to the hundred other good ideas that there are. You have to pick carefully.'

Jobs practised this principle rigorously at Apple, often streamlining product lines and cutting down on projects that were not core to the company's vision. His ability to say no effectively helped Apple focus its resources on creating ground-breaking products like the iPhone, iPad and MacBook.

▪

One of the most famous examples of saying no comes from Mahatma Gandhi's Salt March in 1930. By refusing to comply with British salt laws, Gandhi turned a simple act of defiance into a powerful symbol of resistance. His 'no' was not just a refusal to follow unjust rules but a call for systemic change, inspiring millions to challenge colonial oppression.

By focusing on fewer, more meaningful pursuits, we avoid the trap of being busy for the sake of being busy and instead cultivate a life that is rich in purpose and fulfilment.

If we do not prioritize our life, someone else will.

I hope you enjoy reading this book as much as I have enjoyed writing it.

In case you have not enjoyed this book, just say no!

1

Understanding the Psychology behind NO!

In a world that increasingly demands more of our time, energy and attention, learning to say no has become a critical skill. Unfortunately, for many, saying no is laden with anxiety, fear and guilt. From the fear of rejection to the overwhelming need for approval, people often struggle with the decision to decline requests.

The word 'no' is a simple but strong way to set boundaries. It shows what someone values, where they draw the line and what matters most to them. Saying no is a thoughtful decision to turn down something that might not be good for one's well-being or future goals. It helps people save their time and energy for the things and people that truly matter, instead of trying to do everything and wearing themselves out.

In essence, saying no is an act of self-respect. It recognizes the finite nature of one's time and emotional bandwidth, empowering individuals to take ownership of their lives. When used effectively, it enables better time management, improved relationships, and a clearer sense of purpose. Moreover, it fosters a sense of control over one's life, replacing the chaotic demands of others with a more intentional, meaningful existence.

The real challenge isn't just saying no. It is doing it in a clear and confident way, without feeling guilty or afraid. To do this well, you need to understand why refusing feels difficult for many people and learn how to handle those challenges.

Why People Struggle to Say No

Saying no, for many, is an uncomfortable act. The reasons behind this discomfort are complex, often tied to deep-seated fears and social conditioning. Some of the most common reasons people struggle to say no include:

1. **Fear of disappointing others:** Many people feel a strong need to be liked and accepted, fearing that by saying no, they will let others down or create disappointment. This can be a powerful motivator, pushing individuals to say yes even when it goes against their own interests.

   Example: Priya's colleague, Ramesh, asked her to take over his project tasks while he attended a family function. Though she was already struggling to meet her deadlines, Priya couldn't refuse, worrying that Ramesh would be upset. She stayed up late for days, became exhausted, and still couldn't meet her own deadlines. She realized later that saying yes hadn't helped anyone.
2. **Fear of rejection:** At the heart of many people's inability to say no lies the fear of rejection. It often stems from a deep-seated psychological need for

connection and belonging. The fear of being rejected by peers, loved ones or colleagues drives many individuals to say yes even when it goes against their best interests. In essence, they say yes not because they want to, but because they fear what might happen if they don't.

Example: When Neha's friends planned a weekend trip, she wanted to say no because she had an important exam coming up. However, she feared they would stop inviting her to future plans if she refused. Reluctantly, she went on the trip but returned feeling stressed and underprepared for her exam. Neha later learned that true friends respect one's priorities.

3. **Guilt:** This is another driving factor in the inability to say no. Individuals may feel they are being selfish or unkind by refusing a request, especially if the person asking is a loved one or someone in need. The desire to be seen as helpful and generous often overrides the personal need for boundaries. Managing guilt effectively requires reframing how we view saying no. Rather than seeing it as an act of selfishness, individuals must learn to see it as an act of self-preservation. Saying no allows individuals to protect their time, energy, and emotional health, which ultimately benefits both themselves and those around them.

   Example: Arjun always said yes whenever his elderly neighbours asked for errands, even if he was busy. One day, when he finally refused because he had to prepare for a work presentation, he felt guilty for letting them down. Over time, he realized that setting boundaries didn't mean being selfish. It meant being responsible about his time and energy.

4. **FOMO (fear of missing out):** With the rise of social media and the constant bombardment of information about what others are doing, many people experience FOMO, the fear of missing out. They say yes to invitations, projects, or opportunities out of fear that they will miss something important or be left behind.

   Example: Rahul joined multiple extracurricular activities in college because he feared he might miss out on something fun or important. Soon, his schedule became so packed that he hardly had time for studies or relaxation. When his grades began to fall, Rahul realized that saying yes to everything wasn't worth it.

5. **Desire to please:** Some people are natural people-pleasers. They derive satisfaction from making others happy and are willing to sacrifice their own well-being to meet the needs of others. This can make it incredibly difficult to say no, as the act feels like a rejection of the person rather than the request.

   Example: Kavita always agreed to help her colleagues, believing it was her way of being a good team member. One evening, when she had promised her daughter she'd help with schoolwork, a colleague asked her to stay late. Kavita couldn't refuse, disappointing her daughter. This incident made her understand the cost of people-pleasing.

6. **The need for approval:** A second factor contributing to the difficulty in saying no is the human need for

validation. Approval from others can feel like a form of social currency, enhancing our sense of self-worth and belonging. Psychologists often explain that the need for validation is rooted in the basic human drive for love, acceptance and inclusion. The danger arises when the need for approval leads individuals to compromise their personal values, priorities or well-being.

Example: Sanjay believed that agreeing to every request at work would earn him the respect and approval of his boss. He took on so many tasks that he struggled to complete them all on time. Surprisingly, when he started saying no to extra work and focused on fewer tasks, his performance improved, and his boss appreciated his efficiency more.

7. **Cultural and social expectations:** Many cultures place a high value on selflessness, encouraging individuals to put others' needs ahead of their own. This societal pressure can make saying no feel countercultural or even rebellious, further compounding feelings of guilt and fear.

   Example: Rekha was raised in a household where women were expected to always be accommodating. When she declined to help with an extra community event because she was already overloaded, some family members criticized her. However, Rekha stood firm and explained that she needed to focus on her commitments first. Over time, they began to respect her choices.

8. **Fear of conflict:** For some, the prospect of saying no brings with it the fear of conflict or confrontation.

They worry that by refusing a request, they will create tension or upset the other person, leading to uncomfortable interactions.

Example: Whenever Manish's relatives asked for favours, he would say yes to avoid conflict, even if it inconvenienced him. One day, he politely declined a request, fearing a confrontation. To his surprise, the relatives accepted his refusal without any argument. Manish learned that not all disagreements lead to conflict.

These reasons reflect a common misconception that saying no is inherently negative, selfish, or harmful. However, learning how to say no in a healthy, respectful way can help alleviate these fears and lead to better outcomes for both parties.

The Negative Impact of Always Saying Yes

Always saying yes can cause many problems for both a person and their relationships. When people take on too much, it affects the quality of their work, relationships and well-being. Some of the biggest downsides of always agreeing to everything are:

1. **Burnout:** The quickest and most noticeable result of always saying yes is burnout. When people take on too many responsibilities, they feel overwhelmed and drained, which affects their body, mind, and emotions. Burnout lowers productivity, increases stress and harms overall health.

   Example: Meena, a school-teacher, constantly agreed to take on additional responsibilities, thinking it was her duty. After months of handling extra tasks, she began feeling exhausted, both mentally and physically. When she finally consulted a doctor, she was told she was experiencing burnout. Meena then decided to limit her commitments and prioritize her health.

2. **Resentment:** Saying yes out of obligation or fear often leads to feelings of resentment. When individuals continuously prioritize others' needs over their own, they may begin to feel taken advantage of or unappreciated. This resentment can damage relationships and lead to passive-aggressive behaviour or withdrawal.

   Example: Whenever Raj said yes to his friends' requests for help, he felt they didn't appreciate his efforts. He began feeling resentful but didn't express it. One day, he realized that by saying yes out of obligation he was harming both himself and his friendships. He started setting boundaries and felt much lighter.

3. **Loss of identity:** When people are constantly saying yes to others' demands, they may lose sight of their own goals, values, and identity. Their lives become a reflection of others' expectations rather than a fulfilment of their own desires, leading to a sense of purposelessness or dissatisfaction.

   Example: Sunita, a young professional, always went along with what her friends or colleagues wanted. She realized one day that she didn't know what she truly wanted in life. By constantly living up to others' expectations, she had lost sight of her own dreams. Sunita started saying no more often, and slowly, she rediscovered her goals.

4. **Reduced quality of work:** When people try to do too much at once, their work quality drops. Handling too many tasks means they can't focus properly on each one, leading to poor results and more stress.

   Example: Vikram, a software developer, accepted every request from his manager to work on additional features. With too many projects on hand, he rushed through tasks, and errors became frequent. After an honest discussion with his manager, Vikram started focusing on fewer tasks, and the quality of his work improved significantly.

5. **Damaged relationships:** Ironically, saying yes too often can also harm relationships. When individuals feel obligated to agree to every request, they may grow resentful or exhausted, which can negatively impact their interactions with others. Additionally, overcommitting often leads to broken promises, as individuals struggle to meet the demands placed on them.

   Example: Ananya always agreed to help her best friend with her studies, even when she had her own exams. One day, when she couldn't keep her promise, her friend felt let down. Ananya realized that by overcommitting, she had unintentionally damaged their friendship. She learned to only agree when she could truly help.

Fear of rejection, if we do not say yes, is often reinforced by societal pressures. Society places great emphasis on consensus, teamwork and cooperation, which often leads individuals to feel that saying no is an act of selfishness or non-cooperation. However, saying yes out of fear can erode one's mental and emotional well-being over time.

How to Say No Effectively

The key to saying no is in how you express it. You don't need to be rude or create conflict when doing so. It can be done politely, respectfully and clearly. Here are some tips to help you say no in a better way:

1. **Be clear and direct:** If your answer is unclear, people might get confused or try to convince you to say yes. A short, firm 'No' or 'I can't' usually works well to show your limits.

   Example: When Rohit's manager asked him to work on a weekend, he directly replied, 'I'm sorry, but I have personal commitments.' His clear and direct response avoided further pressure, and the manager respected his boundary without asking again.
2. **Suggest alternatives:** If appropriate, offer an alternative solution or suggest a compromise. If you cannot attend an event, you might suggest meeting up at another time. This shows that you still value the relationship while maintaining your boundaries.

   Example: When Akash was invited to a friend's wedding but couldn't attend due to work, he said, 'I won't be able to join the wedding, but I would love to catch up later. How about dinner next weekend?' His friend appreciated the gesture and accepted the alternative plan.

3. **Be honest, but kind:** Being honest is important when saying no, but it's also good to be kind. You can give a simple reason without too much detail, like saying, 'I'm focusing on my personal projects right now, so I can't take on anything new.'

   Example: When Shweta's cousin asked her to contribute to an event she couldn't attend, she replied, 'I wish I could, but my schedule is packed. I hope you have a wonderful event!' Her honest yet kind response was well received, and there were no hard feelings.
4. **Practise saying no:** Saying no gets easier with practice. It is always good to start with small, low-stakes situations, and gradually work your way up to more significant requests.

   Example: Aarav started small by declining unnecessary sales calls and minor requests from acquaintances. Gradually, he gained confidence and was able to say no to bigger demands at work and in personal life, helping him feel more in control and less stressed.

▪

In the Bible, Jesus advises against seeking approval from others in his Sermon on the Mount. He says, 'Beware of practising your righteousness before other people in order to be seen by them, for then you will have no reward from your Father who is in heaven.'[1] This teaching underscores the idea that seeking approval from others is fleeting and that true fulfilment comes from living in alignment with one's values and principles.

Saying no is an important skill that helps people take care of themselves, set limits and stay true to what matters most to them. But it can be hard to say no because people often fear being rejected, wanting others to like them, or feel guilty afterward. By learning why these feelings happen and how to manage them, people can become more confident in saying no when needed.

Overcoming the fear of rejection requires accepting that rejection is a normal part of life and does not diminish one's worth. Addressing the need for approval involves cultivating self-worth from within rather than seeking validation from others. Finally, managing guilt requires recognizing that saying no is not an act of selfishness but an act of self-care.

By mastering the art of saying no, individuals can reclaim their personal agency, make decisions that align with their values, and live more fulfilling and authentic lives. As Ayn Rand aptly puts it in *The Fountainhead*, 'The question isn't who is going to let me; it's who is going to stop me.'

The power to say no is, ultimately, the power to shape one's own life.

▪

In today's fast-paced world, the ability to say no is a crucial skill that many struggle to master due to deep-seated fears, guilt and societal conditioning.

---

[1]Bible, Matthew 6:1, ESV.

It is important to understand that saying no empowers individuals to prioritize their long-term goals over the constant demands placed on them. At its heart, it is about consciously protecting one's time, energy and emotional bandwidth, which can lead to better time management, healthier relationships and a more purposeful life.

It is important to delve into psychological reasons behind the discomfort in saying no. We must also be aware of the negative consequences of always saying yes, such as burnout, resentment and loss of personal identity. Overcommitting often results in reduced quality of work and damaged relationships, as individuals feel stretched too thin. Ironically, constantly agreeing to requests can lead to broken promises and strained connections.

In conclusion, I hope that readers embrace the art of saying no as a tool for reclaiming control over their lives. By overcoming the fear of rejection, letting go of the constant need for approval and reframing guilt as an unnecessary burden, individuals can foster a more balanced, intentional existence both at work and in their personal lives.

2

Why We Struggle to Say No!

The mind acts according to desires, which
are like restless waves.
Bound by attachment, man struggles to
distinguish between duty and desire.

—Bhagavad Gita 2.62

At its core, the word 'no' is a powerful boundary-setting tool that communicates one's values, limits and priorities. It signals a conscious choice to decline something that may not serve a person's well-being or long-term goals. It allows people to conserve their energy for the commitments and relationships that matter most, rather than stretching themselves thin by agreeing to every request.

In our daily lives, the struggle to say no is a universal experience. Whether it is agreeing to tasks at work, attending social events or accommodating the needs of friends and family, we often find ourselves saying yes when we want to say no. This inability to refuse stems from a complex interplay of cultural, emotional, psychological and societal factors. Exploring these dimensions can illuminate why saying no is so difficult, and how embracing the power of refusal can lead to healthier, more balanced lives.

Learning to refuse recognizes the finite nature of one's time and emotional bandwidth, empowering individuals to take ownership of their lives. When used effectively, it enables better time management, improved relationships, and a clearer sense of purpose. Moreover, it fosters a sense of control over one's life, replacing the chaotic demands of others with a more intentional, meaningful existence.

From an early age, we are conditioned to seek approval and avoid conflict. In many cultures, especially those deeply rooted in collectivist values like India's, the word 'no' is often perceived as disrespectful or selfish.

Indic scriptures, such as the Mahabharata and the Bhagavad Gita, provide profound insights into this struggle. In the Gita, Krishna reveals the binding nature of desire and attachment through the quality of *rajas*:

रजो रागात्मकं विद्धि तृष्णासङ्गसमुद्भवम् ।
तन्निबध्नाति कौन्तेय कर्मसङ्गेन देहिनम् ॥[2]

In this light, the desire to please is the source of many entanglements, for it binds one to others' expectations. The restless energy of rajas ensnares the spirit in ceaseless striving for approval, obscuring the serenity that arises from detachment and self-knowledge.

The Indic scriptures sometimes portray women as self-sacrificing figures. Let us look at some well-known stories that illustrate the use of 'no' in some of our scriptures:

1. In the Mahabharata, Yudhishthira exemplifies this challenge. Renowned for his adherence to dharma

---

[2]Bhagavad Gita, 14.7.

(righteousness), his inability to say no to a dice game proposed by his cousins, the Kauravas, leads to disastrous consequences for him and his family. Despite knowing the risks, he agrees out of a sense of duty and familial obligation. His story serves as a cautionary tale, highlighting how the fear of offending others or breaking societal norms can trap us into decisions that harm us in the long run.

2. Think of the story of Sita from the Ramayana. When Ravana, the demon king, abducts her and tries to coerce her into submission, Sita's refusal to yield demonstrates the courage to say no even in the face of great peril. Her steadfastness is inspiring but it also underscores how refusing often requires immense emotional strength and conviction.
3. The story of Karna from the Mahabharata exemplifies this further. His unwavering loyalty to Duryodhana, despite knowing the latter's unjust motives, can be seen as an inability to say no to his benefactor. Karna's fear of breaking his bond with Duryodhana leads him to make decisions that ultimately result in his downfall. His story teaches us the importance of discerning loyalty and setting boundaries.

However, figures like Draupadi from the Mahabharata challenge these norms. When she is humiliated in the Kaurava court, she boldly questions the morality of the assembly. Her refusal to accept injustice inspires strength and defiance against societal expectations. Her story reminds us that saying 'no' is not just a personal act but also a social statement.

In contemporary contexts, working mothers often face similar dilemmas. She might hesitate to refuse additional responsibilities at work for fear of being seen as less committed, even if it means compromising her family time or personal well-being. This double burden of societal expectations and professional demands makes saying no particularly challenging.

But, our scriptures teach us that the act of saying no is deeply transformative. It allows us to reclaim our time, energy, and focus. By refusing what doesn't align with our values or capacities, we create space for what truly matters.

Another anecdote illustrates this point. A close friend once struggled to balance work and personal commitments. She found it difficult to refuse overtime requests, fearing repercussions at work. However, this left her emotionally drained and unable to spend quality time with her family. After attending a workshop on boundary-setting, she began to practise saying no. To her surprise, not only did her colleagues respect her decision, but she also became more effective at work and happier in her personal life.

By embracing the power of 'no' we can align our lives with our values and lead more fulfilling, intentional lives—both personally and professionally.

3

The Consequences of Always Saying YES

As is your will, so is your deed.
As is your deed, so is your destiny

—Brihadaranyaka Upanishad, 4.4.5

In a world driven by productivity, achievement, and social approval, many of us fall into the trap of constantly saying yes to everything. Let us start with some interesting stories from our scriptures which illustrate this concept.

- King Dasaratha's unconditional promise to Kaikeyi to grant her two boons famously led to catastrophic consequences when Kaikeyi manipulated the boons to make Dasaratha send Rama into exile and crown her son, Bharata, as king. Dasaratha's inability to refuse her demand due to his earlier vow caused him immense grief and ultimately led to his death[3].
- Yudhishthira's inability to say no to the game of dice, despite knowing Shakuni's intentions, led to the loss of his kingdom, wealth, and even his brothers

[3]Valmiki Ramayana, Ayodhya Kanda.

and wife. His compulsive agreement stemmed from his adherence to dharma, but it caused immense suffering for the Pandavas[4].

- The Guru Granth Sahib emphasizes discernment and warns against always agreeing with false teachings. A story is recounted about followers who blindly say yes to a fraudulent guru, leading them astray from true spirituality[5].
- Devadatta, Buddha's cousin, was surrounded by followers who always agreed with him, even when his intentions were malevolent. Their blind agreement led him to challenge the Buddha and meet a tragic end[6].
- Chanakya highlights the danger of a king who always agrees with his courtiers out of fear or ignorance. Such rulers lose respect and control over their kingdom[7].

▪

Whether it's a work project, a social event, or a personal favour, the act of consistently agreeing to others' demands without considering personal boundaries can lead to numerous negative outcomes. While saying yes may seem like a way to maintain harmony, make others happy, or achieve success, it often results in the following:

1. Burnout and Stress

---

[4]Mahabharata, Sabha Parva.
[5]Guru Granth Sahib, Ang 953.
[6]Jataka Tales, Devadatta's Betrayal.
[7]Arthashastra, Book 1, Chapter 19.

2. Loss of Identity, and
3. Strained Relationships.

Burnout and Stress: The Physical and Emotional Toll of Overcommitting

One of the harmful consequences of saying yes too often is burnout.

Many individuals feel pressure to take on more responsibilities than they can reasonably handle. Whether it is at work, in social circles, or within family life, the expectation to be constantly available and accommodating can quickly lead to overwhelming stress.

Burnout is a state of chronic physical and emotional exhaustion caused by prolonged stress and over commitment. It is characterized by feelings of fatigue, cynicism, and a lack of accomplishment. According to the World Health Organization (WHO), burnout is an 'occupational phenomenon'. It is often the result of excessive work-related stress. However, burnout can also occur in personal settings, particularly when someone continuously prioritizes others' needs over their own.

The physical symptoms of burnout can be severe, affecting an individual's overall health and well-being. People who constantly say yes may experience:

1. Chronic fatigue and lack of energy
2. Sleep disturbances, including insomnia
3. Increased susceptibility to illness due to a weakened immune system
4. Headaches, muscle tension, and other stress-related physical symptoms

Over time, this can lead to more serious health issues. Constantly saying yes can lead to feelings of resentment, anxiety, and depression. When individuals stretch themselves too thin, they may feel overwhelmed by their commitments, which in turn can result in emotional exhaustion. The inability to say no often stems from a desire to avoid conflict or rejection, but it can also create a sense of helplessness, as the individual feels trapped in a cycle of overcommitment.

Karna's unwavering 'yes' to Duryodhana's every request, even when it was unethical, led to his downfall. His loyalty, though admirable, became his weakness[8].

Consider the case of a 35-year-old marketing executive who prided herself on being dependable and hardworking. She constantly said yes to new projects, meetings, and requests from her boss, even when it meant working late nights and weekends. Over time, she began to experience severe burnout. She suffered from migraines, insomnia, and chronic fatigue, and her performance at work began to decline. Despite her initial enthusiasm, she became disengaged and resentful of her job. Eventually, she had to take a leave of absence to recover from the toll that overcommitting had taken on her health.

This story is not unique.

Many professionals in high-stress environments experience similar outcomes when they fail to set boundaries. The culture of constant availability, especially in competitive industries, can lead to severe consequences for both physical and mental health.

---

[8]Bhagavad Gita, Chapter 18.

Loss of Identity: How Saying YES Can Lead to a Loss of Self-Identity

Another significant consequence of always saying yes is the gradual erosion of personal identity. When individuals prioritize others' needs and desires over their own, they risk losing touch with their own values, goals, and preferences. Over time, this can lead to a loss of self-awareness and a diminished sense of individuality.

For many people, the inability to say no is rooted in a desire to please others. They may fear disappointing others, being perceived as selfish, or missing out on opportunities. However, by constantly accommodating others' demands, individuals may begin to shape their lives around external expectations rather than their own desires. This can result in a life dictated by others, where personal goals are sidelined in favour of fulfilling others' requests.

Over time, saying yes to everyone else's agenda can lead to a blurred sense of self.

Guru Granth Sahib advises that blind obedience without understanding is akin to walking in darkness. Always agreeing without reflection leads to spiritual stagnation[9].

Individuals may lose sight of their own passions, interests, and long-term aspirations. Instead of pursuing personal growth, they become defined by their ability to meet others' expectations. This loss of identity can be particularly harmful in both personal and professional contexts.

Bhishma's vow to remain celibate and never claim the throne was a result of his father's desire to marry Satyavati.

---

[9]Guru Granth Sahib, Ang 1245.

His inability to challenge his father's wishes set in motion a series of events that led to the Kuru dynasty's eventual destruction[10].

Let us take the example of a talented graphic designer who started his own freelance business. Initially, he was passionate about creative projects that aligned with his artistic vision. However, as his business grew, he found himself saying yes to every client request, even when the projects did not align with his personal interests. Over time, his work became driven by his clients' demands rather than his own creative vision. He began to feel disconnected from his passion for design and found himself creatively unfulfilled. His identity as a designer became diluted, and he no longer felt in control of his career.

The long-term effects of losing one's identity can be profound. When individuals are no longer in touch with their own values and desires, they may experience feelings of dissatisfaction, frustration, and emptiness. This can lead to a sense of purposelessness, where individuals feel like they are living someone else's life rather than their own.

In extreme cases, the loss of identity can lead to a crisis of self-worth. Individuals may begin to question their value and relevance, especially if they define themselves solely by their ability to meet others' expectations. The constant act of saying yes can become a form of self-sabotage, where individuals sacrifice their own needs for the sake of others.

---

[10]Mahabharata, Adi Parva.

Strained Relationships: The Hidden Cost of Saying YES Too Often

While saying yes may seem like a way to maintain harmonious relationships, it can lead to significant strain in personal and professional connections. When individuals agree to too many commitments, they often spread themselves too thin, leading to resentment, frustration, and imbalance in relationships.

One of the most common consequences of overcommitting is the development of resentment. Individuals who constantly say yes may feel taken advantage of or unappreciated, especially if their efforts go unnoticed or unacknowledged. This resentment can build over time, leading to passive-aggressive behaviour, frustration, and emotional distance in relationships.

In a workplace setting, an employee who constantly agrees to take on additional tasks may eventually feel overburdened and underappreciated. While they may initially agree to extra work to be seen as a team player, the lack of recognition for their efforts can lead to feelings of resentment towards colleagues or supervisors. This dynamic can damage workplace relationships and create tension within teams.

Similarly, in personal relationships, always saying yes can lead to an imbalance in the give-and-take dynamic. For instance, a person who always agrees to help friends or family members, even at the expense of their own time and energy, may eventually feel used or exploited. This can lead to strained relationships, as the individual becomes frustrated with the perceived lack of reciprocity.

Healthy relationships are built on mutual respect, communication, and balance. When one person constantly says yes it can disrupt this balance, leading to feelings of inequality and frustration. Setting boundaries is essential for maintaining healthy relationships, as it allows individuals to prioritize their own needs while still being available to support others.

In some cases, saying no can strengthen relationships by fostering open communication and mutual understanding. For example, a person who sets clear boundaries with a friend or partner is more likely to have a balanced and fulfilling relationship, where both parties feel respected and valued.

Consider the case of two close friends who have known each other since college. Over the years, one developed a pattern of constantly asking the other for favours, whether it was help with errands, emotional support, or last-minute assistance with work projects. Initially, the friend was happy to help, but as the requests became more frequent, she began to feel overwhelmed. Despite her growing frustration, she continued to say yes out of fear of damaging the friendship.

Eventually, her resentment reached a breaking point, and she confronted her friend about the imbalance in their relationship. While the conversation was difficult, it ultimately led to a healthier dynamic, where both friends were able to set clearer boundaries and communicate their needs more effectively.

▪

While saying yes may seem like a way to be helpful, maintain harmony, or achieve success, the consequences of overcommitting can be profound. Burnout and stress, loss of identity, and strained relationships are just some of the negative outcomes that arise when individuals fail to set boundaries and prioritize their own well-being. Buddha warned against the extremes of always saying yes or no, teaching that balance and discernment are key to avoiding unnecessary suffering[11]. Learning to say no is a crucial skill for maintaining balance and protecting one's physical, emotional, and mental health.

By setting boundaries and being selective about commitments, individuals can regain control over their lives, preserve their sense of self, and build healthier, more fulfilling relationships. Ultimately, the power of saying no lies in its ability to create space for personal growth, self-care, and authentic connections with others.

In conclusion, inspired by Buddha's teachings, saying No is not about rejection but about creating space for personal growth, self-care, and authentic connections. By embracing the power of 'no' individuals can achieve fulfilment, preserve their identity, and foster meaningful relationships at work and in life. This vital skill empowers readers to live intentionally and with purpose.

---

[11]Dhammapada, Chapter 14.

4

The Benefits of Saying No

Let your aims be common, and your
hearts of one accord,
and all of you be of one mind, so
you may live well together

—Rig Veda 10.191.4

It is often difficult to refuse requests or opportunities, as many of us are conditioned to equate saying no with negativity, selfishness, or missed chances. However, the contrary could be also true. Saying no, when done mindfully, may be seen as an act of self-care, self-discipline, respect, and empowerment.

The Vedas encourage harmonious living by urging individuals to say no to discord and selfishness. A village leader, by saying no to favouritism and instead aligning with collective goals, ensured the prosperity of his community, demonstrating the power of boundaries in leadership[12].

Steve Jobs famously said that people think focus means saying yes to the thing you have got to focus on. But that is

---

[12]Rig Veda 10.191.4.

not what it means at all. It means saying no to the hundred other good ideas that there are. You have to pick carefully.

Jobs understood that focus requires ruthless prioritization, not just an ability to identify the right tasks, but the courage to decline the wrong ones. His success in building Apple into one of the world's most innovative companies was due in large part to his practice of saying no to numerous initiatives, allowing him to direct resources toward only a few key projects that would yield the greatest impact.

Let us discuss the benefits of saying no.

Reclaiming Your Time

One of the most immediate benefits of saying no is that it allows individuals to reclaim their time and exercise greater control over how they spend it. Time, unlike most other resources, is finite and irreplaceable. Every 'yes' given to something unimportant is time taken away from things that matter, whether it be personal goals, family, rest, or self-improvement.

'The wise who know the self, the unchanging reality, say "NO" to desires and transcend the illusion of the material world[13].' A seeker struggling with worldly temptations found solace in the teachings of the Upanishads. By learning to say no to fleeting pleasures, they discovered inner peace and focus on their spiritual growth.

Saying no to tasks or obligations that detract from personal purpose helps maintain this focus and clarity. When we reclaim our time through the power of refusal, we also

---

[13]Mundaka Upanishad 3.2.6.

cultivate a sense of urgency and freedom. Instead of being reactive, constantly accommodating others' expectations, we become proactive, directing our energy toward activities that foster growth, satisfaction, and fulfilment.

'An intelligent person should say no to pleasures that compromise long-term goals.'[14] Chanakya advised Chandragupta Maurya to refuse short-term luxuries to focus on building a robust empire. This discipline laid the foundation for the Mauryan dynasty's greatness.

Enhanced Focus and Productivity

Another significant benefit of saying no is the enhancement of focus and productivity. Every time we say yes to something, we dilute our focus and scatter our efforts. The human brain thrives on focus. Multitasking or managing too many commitments at once leads to diminished effectiveness.

'Rama says no to the golden deer, understanding it to be an illusion that distracts from dharma.'[15] Despite Sita's insistence, Rama was initially reluctant to chase the golden deer, recognizing its deceptive nature. This lesson illustrates the importance of saying no to distractions that can derail one's purpose.

Neuroscientific studies suggest that switching between tasks impairs performance and can lead to cognitive overload, often resulting in a slower completion of tasks or poorer quality work. Saying no is an act of safeguarding one's mental energy and attention.

---

[14]Chanakya, Arthashastra 1.6.3.

[15]Ramayana, Aranya Kanda, Sarga 10.

Saying no can also increase productivity by eliminating distractions. Distractions come in many forms: unnecessary meetings, requests from others, or even well-intentioned offers to collaborate. In the workplace, constant interruptions and competing demands can erode one's ability to perform deep work which would require undisturbed periods of concentration, and the modern work environment—with its constant pings, emails, and meetings—makes this nearly impossible.

By saying no to unnecessary interactions and obligations, individuals can carve out time for uninterrupted work, allowing for deeper focus and higher productivity. Moreover, when we constantly say yes to requests, we not only risk burnout but also deprive ourselves of the opportunity to excel in the tasks that truly matter. A key component of high performance is the ability to manage one's time and energy efficiently, something that is impossible without the strategic use of no.

Improved Mental Health

Saying no also offers significant benefits for mental health, particularly when it comes to setting boundaries and preventing burnout. Constantly prioritizing the needs of others over one's own can lead to emotional exhaustion, resentment, and even mental health issues such as anxiety and depression.

One of the key principles of positive psychology is the importance of self-care and boundary-setting as a means of maintaining mental well-being. Establishing healthy boundaries in relationships and work prevents people from feeling overwhelmed and ensures that they maintain a sense of self-respect and autonomy.

From a psychological standpoint, saying no is empowering because it reinforces an individual's ability to control their circumstances rather than being at the mercy of external demands.

'Renounce falsehood and focus on truth; say no to distractions and immerse in the Name.'[16] A disciple once struggled to concentrate on prayers. Upon renouncing his attachment to worldly distractions, as advised in the Guru Granth Sahib, he found clarity and spiritual fulfilment.

Setting boundaries through refusal also leads to greater resilience and emotional regulation. People who practice saying no develop a stronger sense of self-awareness and are more attuned to their emotional needs. They can recognize when they are reaching their limits and act accordingly, rather than pushing themselves into situations that may exacerbate stress or anxiety.

Moreover, the practice of saying no can improve one's relationships, contrary to the common fear that it may lead to alienation or conflict. When individuals communicate their boundaries clearly and assertively, they foster mutual respect and healthier interpersonal dynamics. People are more likely to respect those who are honest about their limitations, and it encourages a culture of open communication and trust.

Saying no is not an act of selfishness, but one of self-love and emotional protection.

---

[16]Guru Granth Sahib, Ang 474.

Empowerment and Assertiveness

One of the profound benefits of saying no is the empowerment it provides. Saying no requires assertiveness, a key skill in maintaining both personal and professional integrity. Assertiveness, distinct from aggression or passivity, is the ability to express one's needs and desires in a respectful yet firm manner. By saying no, individuals assert their right to make decisions that are in their best interest, rather than being swayed by the expectations or pressures of others.

This sense of empowerment is reflected in ancient philosophical teachings. Greek philosopher, Epictetus stated that we must control what is within our power and let go of what is not, a sentiment echoed in his famous quote, 'Freedom is the only worthy goal in life. It is won by disregarding things that lie beyond our control.'[17]

In the context of saying no, this wisdom suggests that true freedom comes from taking control over our decisions, rather than being controlled by external obligations or societal pressures.

The act of saying no also instils confidence. As individuals become more comfortable with refusing requests, they develop a stronger sense of self-worth and clarity about their priorities. This confidence spills over into other areas of life, leading to a greater sense of empowerment in both personal and professional spheres.

---

[17]Epictetus. *The Art of Living*, trans. Sharon Lebell, HarperOne, 1995.

Cultivating a More Meaningful Life

The power of saying no lies in its ability to help individuals lead more meaningful and purpose driven lives. When we say no to distractions, trivialities, or external demands that do not serve our goals, we open space for the things that truly matter.

'Saying no is as sacred as saying yes. It is an affirmation of your authenticity.'[18] A corporate executive, exhausted by overwork, learned to say no to unreasonable demands. This act of self-preservation helped them achieve a healthier work-life balance and greater respect at work.

Saying no can help individuals align their actions with their core values. Many of us are familiar with the feeling of regret that comes from saying yes to something that doesn't align with our beliefs or priorities.

'A wise person must say no to actions that lead to unrighteousness.'[19] Vidura's counsel to King Dhritarashtra about rejecting adharma exemplifies the courage needed to uphold moral principles even under pressure. When we learn to say no more often, we make room for actions and decisions that resonate with our authentic selves, leading to a greater sense of integrity and inner peace.

▪

In a world where saying yes is often equated with opportunity and positivity, learning to say no can feel counterintuitive. The ability to say no is a crucial skill that fosters self-respect,

---

[18]Osho. *Courage: The Joy of Living Dangerously*, St. Martin's Press, 1999.

[19]Mahabharata, Shanti Parva, Chapter 160.

better time management, improved mental well-being, and empowerment. While many hesitate to refuse requests for fear of appearing selfish or negative, mindful rejection is in reality, an act of self-care and a powerful tool for prioritization.

One of the primary benefits of saying no is the reclamation of time. Time, unlike other resources, is finite. Every unnecessary commitment consumes time that could be invested in personal growth, rest, or crucial tasks. Refusal enables proactive control over one's schedule, transforming a reactive mindset into a deliberate approach to life. Furthermore, by maintaining clarity of purpose through selective engagement, individuals can avoid the overwhelming burden of over commitment, leading to enhanced focus and productivity.

From a neuroscientific perspective, multitasking diminishes cognitive performance. Each new task that garners attention fragments focus and reduces overall effectiveness. Saying no, therefore, is not merely about setting limits but about safeguarding one's mental bandwidth for deep, undisturbed work. Whether in the office or at home, the power to decline unnecessary distractions is directly linked to higher productivity and quality output.

In addition to productivity, mental health benefits immensely from setting boundaries. Constantly prioritizing others' needs can lead to burnout, anxiety, and resentment. Refusal, when done respectfully, serves as a boundary-setting mechanism that upholds personal well-being. It encourages individuals to prioritize self-care and fosters resilience by preventing emotional exhaustion.

Beyond practicality, we must recognize the role of saying no in fostering assertiveness. Being assertive, neither aggressive nor passive, empowers us to communicate our needs firmly while maintaining respect for others.

As the ancient philosopher Epictetus remarked, freedom comes from controlling what lies within our power. Saying no is a pathway to this freedom, granting individuals the confidence to live authentically and intentionally.

In conclusion, cultivating the courage to say no leads to a more purpose-driven life. By eliminating distractions and aligning actions with core values, individuals can lead lives of integrity, fulfilment, and clarity. Whether navigating personal goals or professional challenges, the practice of saying no is an indispensable tool for living meaningfully.

5

'Jugaad' vs Saying No

The power of saying No to limitations, financial or structural, is the birthplace of jugaad, where creativity conquers constraint.

—CK Prahalad

Originating from India, *Jugaad* refers to an innovative, often makeshift solution to a problem, typically executed with limited resources. It is a creative way of making do with what one has to overcome challenges, whether in business, engineering, or everyday life.

On the other hand, the practice of 'Saying No' involves consciously refusing a request, project, or proposal, often for valid reasons such as lack of resources, feasibility, or ethical concerns. Both concepts stand at opposite poles of decision-making processes and yet there are similarities as well.

One criticism of Jugaad is that it may often be a way to say yes when the answer should be no. Jugaad involves doing something or anything rather than opting for the harder but often necessary path of refusal or postponement until better resources or conditions are available.

■

Let us look at the positives and negatives of Jugaad.

Positives of Jugaad

1. *Innovation Under Constraints*: One of the most celebrated aspects of Jugaad is its ability to generate solutions when resources are scarce. This form of improvisation can lead to unconventional innovation. For instance, during the 2001 Gujarat earthquake, villagers constructed makeshift homes using recycled materials like tin sheets and wooden beams. Despite limited financial means, the homes were functional and provided shelter to displaced families.
2. *Speed of Execution*: Jugaad often comes into play when time is of the essence. A good example of this is when the Indian railways needed to keep their communication lines open during heavy monsoons. Engineers used plastic water bottles to float electrical wires over the floodwaters, a makeshift yet functional solution that restored communication rapidly.
3. *Cost-Effectiveness*: By using locally available and often recycled materials, Jugaad reduces costs. This is evident in rural parts of India, where many farmers use inexpensive and locally sourced tools, such as converting old bicycles into water pumps. These hacks can keep businesses or personal projects running without massive financial investment.
4. *Flexibility and Adaptability*: The improvisational nature of Jugaad makes it highly adaptable to changing circumstances. In volatile environments, Jugaad can quickly accommodate new variables. A company

facing a sudden supply chain disruption might use Jugaad to reconfigure its production process to use alternative, readily available materials.

Negatives of Jugaad

1. *Lack of Sustainability*: While Jugaad may offer quick fixes, it is often not a sustainable or long-term solution. It is reactive rather than proactive. For example, using water bottles to float electrical wires is not a long-term infrastructural fix; it only buys time. Overreliance on Jugaad can result in a business model that is not built to scale or to be sustainable over time.
2. *Quality Concerns*: Makeshift solutions often come at the cost of quality. Using recycled materials or quick fixes can lead to subpar products or services. For instance, a company that uses Jugaad to assemble a product might find that its life expectancy is far lower than that of its competitors, resulting in customer dissatisfaction.
3. *Potential Legal or Ethical Issues*: In some cases, Jugaad solutions may skirt regulatory or ethical guidelines. For example, some small-scale manufacturers may bypass safety protocols in their factories by using makeshift tools that do not meet industry standards, thus putting workers at risk.
4. *Short-Term Mindset*: The problem with Jugaad is that it often addresses immediate issues without considering long-term consequences. It can foster a culture of band-aid solutions rather than systemic

improvements. In a company setting, employees who rely too heavily on Jugaad may miss opportunities to optimize processes at a higher, more strategic level.

While Jugaad is useful in emergencies, it can fail in environments where long-term planning, quality control, and scalability are paramount. Established corporations or industries that rely heavily on precision, such as aviation or pharmaceuticals, cannot afford to compromise on safety and quality. In these industries, makeshift solutions could result in catastrophic outcomes.

'Saying no to waste and inefficiency is what drives the Jugaad mindset, forcing us to think creatively with what we have.'[20]

Jugaad could be seen as a diluted form of yes because it postpones difficult decisions and promotes temporary fixes rather than addressing core problems. In some ways, Jugaad operates in a grey area between compliance and defiance.

It is a 'yes, but' or a 'yes, somehow!'

▪

At the same time, there are positives and negatives to 'Saying No'.

The Positives of Saying No

1. *Clarity and Focus*: Saying no allows individuals or organizations to focus on what matters. It promotes better resource allocation and prioritization.

---

[20]Ramesh Mashelkar, Scientist and Innovation Advocate.

2. *Preserving Quality*: Saying no helps maintain high standards. By refusing to engage in half-hearted efforts or subpar projects, companies can protect their reputation and ensure that their output is of consistently high quality. In industries like aerospace or medicine, saying no to shortcuts saves lives and preserves trust.
3. *Long-Term Planning*: When businesses say no to certain opportunities, they make room for better, more strategic decisions down the line. It fosters a mindset of long-term planning and sustainable growth.

The Negatives of Saying No

1. *Missed Opportunities*: There is a fine line between prudent refusal and missed opportunity. Saying no too often can lead to a risk-averse culture that stifles innovation. For example, Kodak's refusal to embrace digital photography, a nascent technology at the time, ultimately led to the company's downfall.
2. *Perceived Inflexibility*: Saying no, especially in a hierarchical or customer-driven context, can sometimes be perceived as inflexibility or lack of customer focus. For example, if a start-up says no to a demanding client because they don't have the resources to deliver, it may lose not only that client but also potential future business from them.

▪

Both Jugaad and saying no have their merits and demerits, depending on the context in which they are used. Jugaad represents ingenuity and resilience but can compromise quality and sustainability. Saying no allows for focus, quality, and long-term planning but can also close the door on potential opportunities.

In an ideal world, a balanced approach would incorporate the best of both. Jugaad should be employed when the situation demands creativity under constraints, but with an eye toward transitioning to more permanent, scalable solutions. Similarly, saying no should be viewed not as a refusal to innovate but as a strategic decision to focus resources where they matter most.

'The art of Jugaad lies in knowing when to say no to conventional paths and creating your own unique solutions instead,'[21] says Navi Radjou, author of *Jugaad Innovation.*

Both approaches require wisdom, foresight, and a keen understanding of the situation at hand. By knowing when to apply Jugaad and when to say no, individuals and organizations can navigate the complexities of modern challenges while ensuring both immediate results and long-term success.

Jugaad and saying no are interconnected as they both demand prioritization and deliberate rejection of inefficiency, over complexity, or unnecessary steps. Saying no is essential to cultivating frugality and focus, the core of Jugaad, which turns constraints into innovation opportunities.

▪

[21]Navi Radjou, Jaideep Prabhu, and Simone Ahuja. *Jugaad Innovation: Think Frugal, Be Flexible, Generate Breakthrough Growth,* Jossey-Bass, 2012.

The concept of Jugaad, rooted in Indian culture, embodies creative problem-solving using minimal resources. Whether in business, daily life, or during crises, it showcases human ingenuity and adaptability. On the other hand, the practice of 'Saying No' represents deliberate decision-making, often driven by a need for resource management, feasibility, or ethical concerns. Both approaches offer valuable lessons in decision-making, though they stand on opposite ends of the spectrum.

Jugaad thrives in environments of constraint, fostering quick, cost-effective solutions. History provides numerous examples where Jugaad proved invaluable. However, while Jugaad excels in emergencies, it often lacks sustainability, quality, and long-term viability. Solutions born from Jugaad may not meet industry standards, risking legal and ethical compliance. Over-reliance on such improvisation can encourage a short-term mindset, hindering systemic improvements and scalability.

In contrast, saying no fosters clarity, focus, and quality.

Refusing to engage in projects that cannot meet high standards helps organizations maintain their reputation and sustain long-term growth. In industries such as aerospace and healthcare, where precision and safety are non-negotiable, the ability to say no to shortcuts can prevent catastrophic outcomes.

Moreover, saying no ensures better resource allocation and long-term strategic planning. Yet, this approach also carries risks. Being too conservative can lead to missed opportunities, as illustrated by Kodak's failure to embrace digital technology, which ultimately led to its decline. Additionally, excessive refusal can create a perception of rigidity, potentially alienating stakeholders.

The key takeaway for individuals and organizations is to balance these approaches. Jugaad, when used judiciously, can provide creative solutions under immediate constraints. However, transitioning to permanent, scalable solutions is essential to sustain success. Meanwhile, saying no should not be viewed as an end to innovation but rather as a strategic tool for focusing on what truly matters. The wisdom lies in discerning when to innovate through Jugaad and when to prioritize long-term goals by saying no.

By embracing the best of both worlds, readers can apply these lessons to their personal and professional lives. Whether it's improvising in challenging situations or making tough decisions to ensure sustainability, knowing when to say yes creatively and when to say no strategically can lead to more effective and thoughtful decision-making.

6

The Art of Saying No in Personal Relationships

Let your Yes be Yes and your No be No

—The Bible, Matthew 5:37

Saying no can often feel like an impossible task, especially when it involves people we care about, be they family, friends, or close acquaintances.

Society frequently encourages us to be agreeable and cooperative, and this inclination can make it difficult to decline requests or set boundaries. However, the inability to say no can lead to feelings of resentment, being overwhelmed and emotional burnout.

Learning the art of saying no is not only vital for our mental well-being but also for maintaining balanced and healthy relationships. This essay will explore strategies for saying no while maintaining healthy relationships, navigating social obligations, and dealing with manipulative tactics designed to elicit a yes.

Setting boundaries in personal relationships is often seen as one of the most challenging aspects of communication. We worry that saying no will hurt feelings, cause misunderstandings, or jeopardize our bonds with loved ones. Yet, it is essential to recognize that boundaries are an integral part of maintaining healthy and fulfilling relationships. Without clear limits, we risk feeling overwhelmed, underappreciated, and emotionally drained.

'Lord Rama never strayed from the path of dharma, even when it meant rejecting the throne or banishing Sita.' Rama's life is a testament to prioritizing values over desires. His decisions to uphold dharma, even at great personal cost, show how saying no can sometimes protect larger principles. In relationships, this teaches us to stand by what is right, even when pressured to compromise.

Unfortunately, not everyone will respect your boundaries, and some may use manipulation tactics to elicit a yes. Recognizing these tactics and knowing how to counter them is crucial for preserving your mental and emotional well-being.

Let us discuss the following points which could be interesting pointers to how we can politely say no.

The Importance of Clear Communication

One of the primary strategies for setting boundaries is clear communication.

When expressing a no, it is essential to be both honest and considerate. Consider a scenario where a family member consistently asks for financial help, but you feel uncomfortable providing it.

You could say, 'I understand that you're in a tough situation, but I'm unable to assist you financially right now. I can help you find resources or someone else who might be able to support you.'

Mothers often have expectations about how their children should behave or live. For instance, when a mother insists on you taking a specific career path, saying no might feel like disobedience. You could say, 'Mom, I know you want the best for me, but I need to follow my own dreams to grow and learn.' The Bhagavad Gita teaches us, 'It is better to live your own destiny imperfectly than to live an imitation of somebody else's life with perfection.'[22] This reminds us that individuality must be respected.

Clear communication does not have to be harsh or abrasive. The key is to assert yourself without leaving room for guilt or doubt. Setting boundaries is not about building walls; rather, it is about creating 'gates' that allow for healthy exchanges while protecting your emotional and mental well-being.

Fathers often give advice that may not always resonate. If a father insists on a traditional way of handling things, a polite refusal could be, 'Dad, I respect your experience, but I would like to try a different approach.' The Mahabharata teaches us that wisdom comes from experience and reflection, but decisions must ultimately be our own.

Communicating your 'no' kindly and assertively can foster respect and understanding in relationships rather than creating tension.

'Do not associate with a fool who always demands and never gives.'[23] This Tamil scripture highlights the wisdom of setting boundaries to avoid being drained by unreasonable demands.

---

[22]Bhagavad Gita, 3.35.

[23]Tirukkural, Verse 82.

Using 'I' Statements

Another valuable tool when setting boundaries is using 'I' statements, which express how you feel without placing blame on the other person.

For instance, if a friend frequently drops by unannounced, instead of saying, 'You always show up without telling me,' you can say, 'I feel overwhelmed when I don't know when to expect company. I would appreciate it if you could give me a heads-up before coming over.'

Children may sometimes ask for more than what is reasonable. A firm yet loving response could be, 'I understand you want this, but it's not something we can do right now.' The Bible advises, 'Train up a child in the way he should go; even when he is old, he will not depart from it.'[24]

This approach reduces the likelihood of the other person feeling attacked or criticized while still conveying your boundary clearly.

Prioritizing Your Well-Being

One of the first steps in navigating social obligations is prioritizing your own well-being.

If attending a gathering or taking on a social commitment will result in stress or exhaustion, it is important to recognize that saying no is an act of self-care, not selfishness.

If your spouse insists on attending a social gathering and you feel drained, you might say, 'I need some time to recharge. Please go ahead without me.' This response reflects

---

[24]Bible, Proverbs 22:6.

the teaching in the Bhagavad Gita: 'A balanced mind is necessary for a balanced life.'

When a child wants you to attend multiple events, but you're overwhelmed, you can say, 'I'd love to be there for everything, but I need to take care of myself too.' This aligns with the wisdom of self-care taught by Jiddu Krishnamurthy: 'In the pursuit of fulfilling everyone else's desires, don't forget your own well-being.'

'Speak the truth; practice righteousness.'[25] Honesty is central to meaningful relationships. Saying no when necessary is part of practicing righteousness. For instance, refusing a friend's unreasonable request may feel difficult but ultimately fosters respect and mutual understanding, promoting a relationship grounded in truth.

An example of this can be seen in the story of a young professional who constantly found herself attending every social event to avoid disappointing her friends. After months of feeling depleted, she realized she needed to start setting limits. She began by politely declining some invitations, explaining that she needed time to recharge. To her surprise, her friends understood, and she was able to maintain her social relationships without sacrificing her own well-being.

Polite Decline

Learning how to politely decline an invitation is crucial. A direct and respectful response can go a long way in ensuring that your relationships remain intact. Instead of saying a blunt

[25]Taittiriya Upanishad 1.11.1.

no to a dinner party invite, you might say, 'Thank you so much for inviting me. I've had a busy week and need some downtime, but I hope to join you next time.' By showing appreciation for the invitation and offering an alternative, you are more likely to avoid offending the host and getting invited a second time.

Your father may want you to join the family business, but if it's not your interest, you could say, 'Dad, I know this business means a lot to you, but I want to pursue my passion. I hope you can support me in that.' Osho once said, 'The greatest courage is to be true to oneself.' Staying true to your calling is essential for personal fulfilment.

'It is far better to discharge one's prescribed duties, even though faultily, than another's duties perfectly.'[26] This verse underscores the importance of staying true to one's path and responsibilities. In personal relationships, this can mean setting boundaries and saying no to actions that do not align with one's purpose. Arjuna's dilemma illustrates how saying no can sometimes be an act of self-respect and adherence to dharma, even if it causes temporary discomfort.

One useful technique is what social psychologists refer to as the 'broken record technique', where you consistently but politely repeat your boundary. For example, if someone continues to pressure you after you have already declined an invitation, you can calmly repeat your initial response. This technique works because it demonstrates your firm stance while maintaining politeness.

---

[26]Bhagavad Gita, 3.35.

Offering Alternatives

Another strategy is to offer alternatives when saying no.

If you are unable to attend a friend's gathering, you could suggest meeting for coffee or catching up at a later date. This not only softens the blow of the refusal but also shows that you value the relationship.

When a spouse suggests a large purchase that you are uncomfortable with, you could respond, 'I see why you want it, but I think we should reconsider our finances.' Chanakya's wisdom emphasizes frugality: 'The wise spend what they can afford and save for what they cannot foresee.'

'Before you start some work, always ask yourself: Why am I doing it?'[27] This advice emphasizes introspection before action. In relationships, saying no thoughtfully can save time and energy. Chanakya's strategic refusals in statecraft demonstrate the importance of deliberate decision-making in fostering respect and trust.

It's a way of affirming the connection without overcommitting yourself.

Guilt-Tripping

One of the most common tactics used to get a yes when you clearly want to decline is guilt-tripping. Guilt-trippers use your sense of obligation and responsibility to make you feel bad for saying no. For example, a family member might say, 'After everything I have done for you, how can you not help me out with this?'

---

[27]Chanakya Neeti.

Sometimes, a mother may try to guilt-trip you into doing something. Responding calmly, you could say, 'Mom, I appreciate your love, but I cannot do this right now.' Jiddu Krishnamurthy said, 'Love is not about control; it is about freedom.' This can be a reminder that healthy relationships allow space for personal choice.

The intent is to evoke feelings of guilt and force compliance. To counter this, it is essential to recognize manipulation and firmly stick to your decision. A response like, 'I understand that you're upset, but I cannot help with this right now,' acknowledges their feelings while maintaining your boundary.

Emotional Blackmail

Emotional blackmail is another tactic used by manipulative individuals to get their way.

Sometimes, people close to you may use emotional manipulation to get their way. Respond by saying, 'I understand that you're upset, but I have to make this decision for myself.' *The Upanishads* emphasize inner clarity: 'The self-realized soul remains unmoved by praise or blame, unaffected by emotional tides.'

If relatives frequently visit without prior notice, disrupting your routine, you might say, 'We love having you over, but it would be helpful if you let us know in advance so we can plan better.' The Bible advises, 'Let your foot be seldom in your neighbour's house, lest he have his fill of you and hate you,'[28] teaching us the value of balance in relationships.

---

[28]Bible, Proverbs 25:17.

They might exaggerate the consequences of your refusal, such as saying, 'If you don't come to my party, it will be ruined,' or, 'If you don't help me, I don't know what I'll do.'

These statements are designed to instill fear and anxieties, making you feel responsible for the other person's emotional state. In these situations, it is important to remind yourself that you are not responsible for managing other people's emotions.

You can say, 'I'm sorry you feel that way, but I cannot attend,' and leave it at that.

Flattery and Bribery

Flattery and bribery are subtler forms of manipulation that may make it difficult to recognize when you are being coerced.

Someone might shower you with compliments or offer favours in exchange for your compliance. While flattery may feel good in the moment, it's important to stay grounded and remember your initial reasoning for saying no.

'He who is unable to protect himself cannot protect others.'[29] This wisdom highlights the importance of self-care and setting boundaries. Just as Yudhishthira learns to balance his duties with personal limits, saying no to protect one's mental and emotional well-being is essential for maintaining healthy relationships.

Stick to your boundaries, and do not let external praise sway your decision.

---

[29]Mahabharata, Udyoga Parva.

The Power of Delayed Responses

When faced with a request or invitation, it's often helpful to delay your response rather than answering immediately. For instance, saying, 'Let me think about it and get back to you,' gives you time to evaluate whether you truly want to say yes or if it's better to decline.

This approach allows you to avoid making impulsive decisions out of guilt or pressure.

Role-Playing and Rehearsing

If saying no feels particularly difficult, rehearsing your response in advance can be helpful.

Role-playing with a trusted friend or practising in front of a mirror can give you the confidence needed to assert yourself in real-time.

'A no uttered with deepest conviction is better than a yes merely uttered to please.' Osho teaches that genuine connections are built on authenticity. Saying no from the heart fosters trust and prevents resentment, while false compliance can corrode relationships over time.

The more you practise, the more natural it will feel to say no when necessary.

Staying Firm but Respectful

Sometimes, people may persist in trying to change your mind, even after you have said no.

If a friend asks for financial help but you can't afford it, say, 'I wish I could help, but I have financial constraints. I hope you understand.' Chanakya once said, 'Never jeopardize your stability for the sake of temporary relief.' This highlights the importance of safeguarding your financial well-being.

'I will not submit to this injustice.'[30] Draupadi's refusal to accept humiliation teaches the power of asserting one's rights. Her stance inspires individuals to say no to disrespect and injustice in personal relationships.

In these cases, staying firm is crucial. Repeat your boundary, if necessary, but remain respectful in your tone and delivery. Over time, people will come to respect your decisions more when they see that you are consistent and unwavering in your responses.

The Emotional Benefits of Saying No

Saying no can have significant emotional benefits. It reduces stress, preserves your energy, and ensures that you are prioritizing your own needs. Overcommitting often leads to feelings of resentment and frustration, which can damage relationships in the long run.

By practicing the art of saying no, you protect your emotional well-being and foster healthier, more respectful connections with others.

The art of saying no in personal relationships is a crucial skill that can enhance both your personal well-being and the health of your relationships. By setting boundaries, navigating social obligations, and recognizing manipulative tactics, you can maintain stronger, more fulfilling relationships without sacrificing your own needs.

---

[30]'Draupadi', The Mahabharata, Sabha Parva.

A friend may often offload their emotional burdens without considering your emotional state. A compassionate but firm response could be, 'I care about you, but I'm feeling overwhelmed right now. Let's talk another time.'

Jiddu Krishnamurthy advised, 'Real friendship is based on freedom, not obligation.'

Saying no does not have to be confrontational or negative; when done with clarity, kindness, and respect, it can lead to more honest and balanced connections.

'Why do you listen to falsehood? It only brings pain and suffering.'[31] Accepting what is untrue or burdensome leads to suffering. Saying no to manipulative or unhealthy dynamics preserves one's peace. A Sikh anecdote of Guru Nanak declining corrupt practices exemplifies how rejection can guide others toward truth.

When an angry man hurled insults at the Buddha, he remained calm. The Buddha explained, 'If someone offers you a gift and you decline it, to whom does the gift belong? So too, if I do not accept your anger, it remains yours.'

▪

The ability to say no is an essential skill, particularly in personal relationships where emotions and social expectations often complicate decision-making.

Society emphasizes being agreeable and cooperative, which can lead individuals to struggle with setting boundaries. However, consistently saying yes at the expense of one's well-being fosters resentment, exhaustion, and emotional burnout.

---

[31]Guru Granth Sahib, Ang 1412.

Mastering the art of saying no is critical for mental health and balanced, fulfilling relationships.

Setting boundaries is one of the cornerstones of healthy communication.

Many fear that saying no could jeopardize their relationships, but clear and considerate communication actually fosters respect. When declining requests, using 'I' statements, such as 'I feel overwhelmed when commitments pile up,' it ensures clarity without blame. This approach reduces misunderstandings and helps maintain strong bonds. Furthermore, recognizing and countering manipulation tactics like guilt-tripping and emotional blackmail is crucial. Manipulative behaviours, such as exaggerating consequences or evoking guilt, aim to elicit compliance through fear or obligation. A calm, firm response like, 'I'm sorry you feel that way, but I cannot help right now,' allows you to maintain your boundaries without succumbing to pressure.

Communicating a decline politely is an invaluable skill in managing social obligations. Instead of blunt refusals, expressing gratitude for invitations while offering an alternative, such as suggesting a future meeting, softens the impact of saying no. This method demonstrates that relationship matters, even if you cannot fulfil the current request. Moreover, techniques like the 'broken record' approach, where you consistently but respectfully repeat your boundary, convey firmness without aggression.

Prioritizing personal well-being is not selfish but an act of self-care. Overcommitting to avoid disappointing others often results in burnout, undermining both personal health and relationships. We can relate to scenarios where professionals, overwhelmed by constant social engagements, learned to reclaim their time by politely but assertively setting limits.

The result will always be stronger relationships based on mutual respect and understanding. Offering delayed responses to requests provides time for thoughtful consideration, reducing impulsive decisions driven by guilt or pressure. Role-playing and rehearsing responses can also help individuals build confidence in asserting themselves. Staying firm but respectful when faced with persistent persuasion reinforces personal boundaries, ultimately teaching others to respect your limits.

The emotional benefits of saying no are profound. It reduces stress, preserves energy, and nurtures self-respect. In the long run, learning to set healthy boundaries leads to more honest and balanced connections. By navigating personal relationships with clarity, kindness, and firmness, readers can foster deeper, more respectful bonds while safeguarding their own well-being.

7

Saying No to Yourself

He who conquers himself is greater
than he who conquers a thousand men in battle

—Atharva Veda, 6.45.1

Saying no to yourself is very difficult and yet could be one of the most powerful tools for self-discipline, personal growth, and long-term success.

We have often made our New Year resolutions on the last day of each year and broken these within the very first week of January. This was probably because we had to resist some temptation to diet or push ourselves to lose weight or do something else where we need to impose self-discipline or say no to ourselves.

At its core, saying no to yourself is about cultivating self-discipline, a key trait necessary for achieving personal and professional milestones. It means recognizing short-term temptations and urges and weighing them against your long-term objectives.

For instance, saying no to an extra hour of television in favour of getting enough rest is an act of prioritizing health and productivity. Similarly, resisting the urge to procrastinate by saying no to distractions, like social media, allows us to stay focused and accomplish tasks on time. Or refusing to eat dessert when we are on a diet is equally challenging, especially if we have a sweet tooth. If we value health, saying no to unhealthy food choices is not an act of deprivation but rather a step toward becoming our best self

By controlling these smaller impulses, we build the mental muscles necessary to tackle larger challenges and achieve bigger dreams. When we are clear about what we want and why, it becomes easier to say no to what does not serve us.

Learning to say no is also a practice of self-awareness. It requires knowing what truly matters to us, as well as the habits, behaviours, or distractions that can derail our progress. This awareness often comes from introspection, where we reflect on our priorities and evaluate whether our actions align with our values and goals.

At the core of self-discipline is the ability to delay gratification.

Renowned psychologist Walter Mischel's 'Marshmallow Experiment' famously illustrated the importance of self-control in children who were willing to wait for a second treat instead of consuming one immediately. Those who could delay gratification were found to have better life outcomes, including academic success, health, and social skills. Perhaps the most important conclusion of The Marshmallow Test is that 'will power' is not an inborn trait. The children who couldn't wait and ate the marshmallows simply had not learned the skills the other children used. Once they learned them, they got better at delaying gratification.

Saying no to ourselves teaches us that not all desires need immediate satisfaction. It helps us align with our long-term goals, instils discipline, and promotes mental clarity.

In many ways, it is the foundation of personal growth, ensuring that we focus on what truly matters rather than succumbing to every fleeting temptation.

'Before you start any work, always ask yourself three questions. Why am I doing it, what the results might be, and will I be successful? Only when you think deeply and find satisfactory answers to these questions, go ahead.'[32] Acharya Chanakya

The Advantages of Saying No to Ourselves

1. *Enhanced Focus and Productivity*
   When we say no to distractions, we create space for deep work and meaningful tasks. Saying no to unnecessary social media browsing, binge-watching, or procrastination, for example, enhances our focus and allows us to concentrate on activities that align with our goals. We reclaim our time and energy, both essential for personal and professional growth.

   Vikram was preparing a crucial report due the next day when he received a group message about an online game night. He was tempted to join, as he didn't want to miss out on the fun. However, he chose to finish the report first and rewarded himself by joining the game later. His boss commended him for submitting the report on time, and that appreciation motivated him to prioritize tasks more effectively in the future.

[32]Chanakya Neeti, Chapter 1, Verse 6.

2. *Strengthening of Willpower*
   Saying no to ourselves strengthens our willpower like a muscle. Each time we resist a temptation, whether it is skipping dessert or waking up early instead of hitting the snooze button, we build inner resilience. This strengthens our ability to make tough decisions in the future, where bigger rewards or consequences are at stake.
   Meera had always struggled with waking up early. Each morning, she would hit the snooze button several times before finally dragging herself out of bed. One day, she made a pact with herself: the next time the alarm rang, she would get up immediately without snoozing. Though difficult at first, she stuck to it. Over the weeks, waking up early became a habit, and this simple act of self-control helped her tackle larger challenges with greater confidence.
3. *Alignment with Long-term Goals*
   The ability to say no enables us to prioritize long-term benefits over short-term pleasures. Whether it's resisting the urge to buy unnecessary items or avoiding unhealthy food choices, each decision builds towards achieving broader goals, such as financial independence or physical well-being.
   Amit always dreamed of going on an international vacation but frequently gave in to impulsive shopping sprees. One day, while browsing through an online store, he felt the urge to buy an expensive watch. Before clicking 'Buy Now', he paused and visualized himself standing in front of the Eiffel Tower, a goal he had always wanted to achieve. He closed the tab,

saved the money instead, and within a year, was able to fulfill his travel dream.

4. *Improved Mental and Physical Health*
   Saying no to negative habits, such as overeating, excessive drinking, or avoiding exercise, contributes to better physical and mental health. By exercising self-discipline, we create a healthier lifestyle that enhances both physical stamina and emotional well-being.

Anil was known for his love of junk food. After a health scare, he decided to make a change. Initially, it was hard to resist the tempting aroma of fried snacks at work, but he reminded himself of his goal to lead a healthier life. He started meal prepping and sticking to his plan. Months later, he not only felt healthier but also inspired his colleagues to adopt better eating habits.

The Disadvantages of Saying No to Ourselves

1. *Emotional Discomfort*
   At times, saying no to ourselves can create internal conflict and emotional discomfort. Denying immediate gratification may bring feelings of frustration or even guilt, especially if we are accustomed to indulging in certain pleasures or habits.
   At a family gathering, Ravi's grandmother insisted he have another serving of dessert. While he loved her cooking, he was trying to stick to a healthier lifestyle. Saying no felt uncomfortable, but he gently explained his goals. Though she looked disappointed

initially, she later praised him for his dedication. Ravi realized that emotional discomfort was temporary, but the benefits of self-discipline were lasting.

2. *Perceived Sacrifice*
   Constantly saying no can create a perception of sacrifice or deprivation. If we do not strike a balance, we may begin to feel as though we are missing out on life's pleasures, which can affect our overall happiness and lead to burnout.
   Ananya's friends frequently invited her for late-night outings, but she often declined to maintain her early morning routine. Initially, she felt left out. Over time, she discovered new activities, like early morning yoga and hikes, which brought her joy and peace. She realized that saying no to some things didn't mean missing out—it meant making room for what truly nourished her.
3. *Risk of Over-Control*
   Excessive self-discipline can also lead to a rigid lifestyle where spontaneity and joy are stifled. Striking a balance between enjoying life's small pleasures and maintaining discipline is crucial for overall well-being. Too much self-control can result in stress or even obsessive behaviours, such as orthorexia, where one becomes overly focused on healthy eating to the detriment of their health.

Ravi became so rigid with his diet and workout routine that he started declining all social events involving food. Over time, he noticed that he felt isolated and anxious. Realizing this wasn't sustainable, he began allowing himself occasional indulgences. This balance helped him maintain his discipline while enjoying life's moments without guilt.

Steps to Develop the Ability to Say No to Ourselves

1. *Identify Your Temptations*
   The first step in saying no to yourself is recognizing where you are most vulnerable to temptations. This could be anything from unhealthy food habits to procrastination. Write down these areas and assess their impact on your life. Awareness is the foundation of change.
   'He who is overly attached to his family members experiences fear and sorrow, for the root of all grief is attachment. Thus, one should discard attachment to be happy.'[33]
   Kiran realized that her tendency to procrastinate often stemmed from distractions like social media and random web browsing. She started keeping a journal to track her distractions. Over time, by identifying and reducing these temptations, she became more productive and mindful of her time.
2. *Set Clear Goals*
   Once you have identified the temptations, set specific, measurable and achievable goals to counter them. If your temptation is binge-watching television, your goal might be to limit screen time to two hours a day. Clear goals give structure and purpose to the practice of self-discipline.

---

[33]Chanakya Neeti, Chapter 12, Verse 3.

Osho says, 'Discipline imposed from the outside destroys freedom. Discipline grown within creates freedom.' This is a nuanced take on how inner discipline leads to genuine liberation.

Neha struggled with staying active. She set a goal to walk 10,000 steps daily. She tracked her progress using a fitness app, and soon, walking became a non-negotiable part of her routine. The clear, measurable goal helped her stay consistent and motivated.

3. *Practice Mindful Decision-Making*

   When faced with a temptation, pause and ask yourself, 'Will this bring me closer to my long-term goals, or is this just satisfying a short-term craving?' Mindfulness allows you to act consciously rather than impulsively.

   'Freedom is not the absence of discipline. It is the absence of the self,' said Jiddu Krishnamurthy. This quote highlights the paradox of true freedom being attainable through discipline and self-awareness.

   Arjun loved buying gadgets but often regretted his impulsive purchases. He adopted a new rule: whenever he wanted something, he would wait 48 hours before buying. This pause helped him distinguish between genuine needs and impulsive wants, saving him money and reducing clutter.

4. *Start Small and Build Gradually*

   Saying no does not have to be all-or-nothing practice. Start by denying small temptations and build your self-control gradually. Over time, you will find it easier to say no to bigger challenges.

   Rahul loved sugary tea but knew it wasn't good for

his health. Instead of cutting out sugar entirely, he started reducing it by half. Over a few months, he adapted to drinking tea without sugar, proving that small, gradual changes lead to sustainable habits.

5. *Reward Yourself for Milestones*
   To maintain motivation, it is important to reward yourself for achieving milestones. Whether it is a cheat day after a week of clean eating or a leisurely activity after completing a major task, small rewards help you maintain balance and joy in life.
   Tanya decided to lose 10 kg and committed to a strict workout routine. For every 3 kg she lost, she allowed herself a small reward—whether it was a spa day or a favourite meal. These milestones kept her motivated and made the journey enjoyable.
6. *Seek Support or Accountability*
   Share your goals with a trusted friend or mentor who can keep you accountable. Sometimes, having someone to remind you of your goals or cheer you on can be the extra motivation needed to stay disciplined.
   Rhea wanted to run her first marathon but lacked consistency. She joined a local running group and shared her goal with them. The group's support kept her accountable, and she successfully completed her marathon with cheers from her newfound friends.

Temptations Where We Can Say No

1. *Food and Health Choices*
   We are constantly surrounded by unhealthy

food options that promise instant pleasure but compromise long-term health. Saying no to fast food, sugary drinks, or excessive alcohol can significantly improve our well-being. Scripture often emphasizes moderation in eating.

For instance, The Bible warns, 'Do not join those who drink too much wine or gorge themselves on meat, for drunkards and gluttons become poor, and drowsiness clothes them in rags.'[34]

At her best friend's birthday party, Sara found herself surrounded by a tempting array of cakes and fried snacks. With her marathon training in mind, she politely declined the desserts and opted for healthier options. While it wasn't easy to resist, Sara later felt a sense of accomplishment when she ran her best time during practice the next morning, reinforcing her belief that small acts of discipline lead to big wins.

2. *Time Management and Procrastination*

   Time is one of our most valuable resources and distractions. Social media, TV, and idle gossip constantly pull us away from productive activities. Learning to say no to distractions allows us to focus on what truly matters.

   In The Bible, we are reminded, 'To everything, there is a season, and a time for every matter under heaven,'[35] implying the importance of mindful time allocation.

---

[34]Bible, Proverbs 23:20-21.

[35]Bible, Ecclesiastes 3:1.

3. *Financial Impulses*
   We live in a consumer-driven world where the temptation to buy unnecessary items is rampant. Saying no to impulse spending can lead to financial stability and freedom.
   The Bible, advises, 'Do not store up for yourselves treasures on earth, where moth and rust destroy, and where thieves break in and steal. But store up for yourselves treasures in heaven,'[36] encouraging us to focus on lasting value rather than material indulgence.
4. *Negative Habits and Behaviours*
   Whether it is smoking, gambling, or engaging in toxic relationships, saying no to harmful behaviours is essential for personal growth.

In the Bhagavad Gita, Lord Krishna tells Arjuna, 'The one who has control over the mind is tranquil in heat and cold, in pleasure and pain, and in honour and dishonour.'[37] This highlights the importance of self-mastery over fleeting pleasures.

▪

Saying no to yourself is a vital practice for personal growth and achieving meaningful goals. While it may come with temporary discomfort, the long-term benefits far outweigh the sacrifices.

---

[36]Bible, Matthew 6:19-20.

[37]Bhagavad Gita, 6.7.

It is not about limiting your freedom but rather empowering yourself to make choices that align with your values and aspirations. Whether it is setting boundaries, cultivating discipline, or prasticing self-care, the ability to say no builds a stronger, more resilient you.

It is through these small, consistent acts of self-control that you create the conditions for long-term success and a more fulfilling life. If you can delay gratification in pursuit of your goals, you will be rewarded for your patience and discipline in the long run.

Saying no to fleeting temptations allows us to say yes to the things that truly matter—our health, relationships, and inner peace.

8

No as a Tool for Personal Growth

When the mind becomes still and quiet,
and the senses are brought under control,
one finds the path to inner strength

—Katha Upanishad, 2.1.10

In a society that often equates being busy with productivity and compliance with kindness, the ability to say no is a skill that is frequently undervalued.

Yet, the simple act of refusing can be one of the most powerful tools for personal growth. Saying no is not about rejection or negativity; it is about creating boundaries, honouring your values, and fostering a mindful approach to life.

When used effectively, 'no' becomes a statement of clarity, intention, and self-respect. Let us discuss how saying no helps individuals align with their core values, build self-confidence, and practice mindfulness in decision-making, ultimately enabling them to live more purposeful and authentic lives.

In the Bhagavad Gita, Lord Krishna advises Arjuna to act in alignment with his dharma. Lord Krishna states:

'It is better to live your own destiny imperfectly than to live an imitation of somebody else's life with perfection.'[38]

The Bible also encourages discernment, which is essential for aligning our choices with our values.

'Let your eyes look straight ahead; fix your gaze directly before you. Give careful thought to the paths for your feet and be steadfast in all your ways. Do not turn to the right or the left; keep your foot from evil.'[39]

Focusing on Core Values: Aligning Actions with Purpose

At its core, saying no is a declaration of what matters most. However, every yes is also a no to something else.

It helps individuals prioritize their time, energy, and resources in alignment with their core values and long-term goals. Too often, people say yes out of fear of disappointing others, societal pressure, or the mistaken belief that acceptance equates to approval.

The *Upanishads* emphasize self-awareness and self-respect as key components of spiritual and personal growth. The *Katha Upanishad* states:

'The Self cannot be known by one who is weak, careless, or without inner strength.'[40]

By learning to say no, individuals can ensure that their commitments reflect their true priorities.

1. *Identifying Core Values*

   Core values are the guiding principles that shape how

---

[38]Bhagavad Gita, 3.35.

[39]Bible, Proverbs 4:25-27.

[40]Katha Upanishad, 2.1.12.

we live, work, and interact with others. They might include integrity, family, health, personal growth, or creativity. To effectively use no as a tool for personal growth, individuals must first identify their core values. This self-awareness acts as a compass, guiding decisions and actions.

For example, consider a professional who values family but is constantly overburdened with work obligations. By saying no to extra assignments that encroach on family time, they honour their core value of family and create a more fulfilling balance.

Similarly, an entrepreneur who values innovation might say no to projects that offer financial rewards but lack creative potential, ensuring their work remains aligned with their vision.

2. *NO as a Boundary-Setting Tool*

   Boundaries are critical for maintaining alignment with core values.

   Saying no is a way of drawing a line and safeguarding what truly matters. When someone declines an invitation to an event because it conflicts with their need for rest, they are not rejecting the person who extended the invitation. They are prioritizing self-care, a core value.

Over time, these boundaries build a life that reflects authenticity and purpose.

Building Self-Confidence: Strengthening Self-Respect

Saying no is an act of self-empowerment.

Each time an individual asserts their boundaries, they reinforce their worth and priorities, which fosters self-confidence and self-respect. This transformation begins with recognizing that no is not a selfish act but a form of self-care and respect for others.

1. *Overcoming the Fear of Rejection*
   Many people struggle with saying no because they fear rejection or being perceived as unkind. However, agreeing to things out of guilt or fear undermines self-confidence. When individuals learn to say no with conviction, they shift their mindset from people-pleasing to self-respect.
   For instance, declining to participate in an unnecessary meeting or a project that detracts from one's goals demonstrates respect for one's time and expertise. This assertiveness communicates self-assurance and earns the respect of peers and colleagues. Over time, saying no reinforces a positive self-image and builds the courage to stand by one's decisions.
2. *Cultivating Self-Respect Through Authenticity*
   Saying no authentically strengthens self-respect by aligning actions with beliefs.
   Each no is a commitment to authenticity, a refusal to compromise on what is most important. For example, a student who declines to participate in unethical academic practices honours their integrity, even if it means facing peer disapproval. This self-respect creates a foundation for lasting self-confidence, enabling individuals to face challenges with resilience and clarity.

Practicing Mindfulness: Conscious Decision-Making

Mindfulness, the practice of being present and aware, is an invaluable tool for learning when and how to say no. It encourages individuals to pause, reflect, and make intentional choices that align with their values and needs. Saying no mindfully ensures that decisions are made with clarity rather than impulse or pressure.

Mahatma Gandhi practiced self-restraint by abstaining from indulgent food, possessions, and even speech at times, saying no to excess and fostering simplicity and discipline. By saying no to material and sensory excess he was able to build inner peace and moral strength.[41]

Some techniques for Mindful Decision-Making that we can think about are given below. To effectively say no, individuals can adopt mindfulness techniques that enhance self-awareness and decision-making:

1. *Pause Before Responding*: When faced with a request, take a moment to breathe and consider whether the commitment aligns with your priorities. A simple 'Let me think about it' creates space for reflection.
2. *Identify the Emotional Impulse*: Mindfulness involves recognizing the emotions driving a yes or no. Is the desire to say yes rooted in fear, guilt, or obligation? By understanding these emotions, individuals can make decisions from a place of clarity.
3. *Ask Reflective Questions*: Questions like 'Does this align with my values?' or 'Will this decision bring

---

[41]Mohandas K. Gandhi. *The Story of My Experiments with Truth*. Navajivan Publishing House, 1927.

me closer to my goals?' help us evaluate whether a yes serves their best interests.

4. *Practice Saying NO Gracefully*: Mindful communication is key to declining requests without alienating others. Phrases like 'I appreciate the offer, but I need to focus on other priorities' convey respect while setting boundaries.

The Role of Self-Compassion

Mindfulness also involves self-compassion, which is essential when saying no.

People often feel guilt or self-doubt after declining requests, especially if the response disappoints others. Self-compassion helps individuals accept that their needs and values are valid, reinforcing their ability to say no without regret.

When used strategically, no transforms lives by fostering authenticity, confidence, and mindfulness. It is not a rejection of others but an affirmation of self.

'Say no to the unnecessary so that you can say yes to the essential,'[42] said Osho.

Let us look at how no can lead to personal growth.

1. *The Overcommitted Professional*: A professional who constantly says yes to extra work may find themselves overburdened and stressed. By saying no to nonessential tasks, they regain control over their time and improve their overall effectiveness.

---

[42]Osho. *Courage: The Joy of Living Dangerously.*

2. *The Social Butterfly*: An individual who accepts every social invitation out of fear of missing out may neglect personal downtime. Learning to say no allows them to recharge and engage in activities that bring genuine joy.
3. *The Aspiring Entrepreneur*: A budding entrepreneur who says yes to every opportunity may lose focus on their core business idea. Saying no to distractions helps them channel their energy into building a successful venture.

In each scenario, no acts as a catalyst for alignment, confidence, and mindfulness. It transforms chaotic lives into intentional ones, enabling individuals to live with greater purpose and fulfilment.

Jesus himself modelled the importance of setting boundaries and saying no. Jesus retreats to a solitary place to pray, despite the demands of the crowd. When his disciples urge him to return, he responds:

'Let us go somewhere else—to the nearby villages—so I can preach there also. That is why I have come.'[43]

This example demonstrates that saying no to immediate demands is sometimes necessary to fulfil one's higher purpose.

As the Bhagavad Gita and the Bible remind us, the path to self-realization requires clarity, courage, and discernment. Embracing the power of 'no' allows us to honour our dharma, live with integrity, and achieve a life of balance and fulfilment.

'You have to decide what your highest priorities are and

---

[43]Bible, Mark 1:35-38.

have the courage, pleasantly, smilingly, unapologetically, to say no to other things. And the way to do that is by having a bigger yes burning inside.'[44]

By embracing no, individuals can create meaningful boundaries, prioritize what truly matters, and cultivate a sense of self-worth that transforms not only their lives but also their interactions with others.

No is not just a refusal. It is a powerful affirmation of self.

▪

In our world, where being constantly busy is equated with productivity and compliance with kindness, learning to say no is often undervalued, yet it can be a transformative tool for personal growth. Far from being a negative response, no is a declaration of one's values, boundaries, and purpose, enabling individuals to lead more intentional, authentic lives.

At its heart, saying no reflects clarity and alignment with core values.

Each yes we offer often means a no to something more important. Many people struggle with declining requests due to societal pressure or the fear of disappointing others, leading to an overwhelming cycle of obligations. By learning to say no, individuals reclaim control over their time and energy, ensuring they are channelled toward meaningful pursuits.

The wisdom of ancient scriptures, such as the Bhagavad Gita and the Bible, underscores the value of discernment and alignment with one's purpose. In the Bhagavad *Gita*, Lord Krishna advises acting in accordance with one's dharma,

---

[44]Covey, Stephen R. *The 7 Habits of Highly Effective People.*

emphasizing that living one's truth imperfectly is better than imitating another's life flawlessly. Similarly, the Bible advocates mindful decision-making, reminding us to focus on steadfastness and purposeful action.

To harness the power of no, individuals must first identify their core values, which serve as a compass for decision-making. Whether it's prioritizing family time, pursuing creative endeavours, or safeguarding personal well-being, saying no ensures that actions align with one's authentic self. Boundaries, reinforced by no, protect these priorities, fostering a life of balance and integrity.

Saying no also builds self-confidence and self-respect. Each time a person asserts their boundaries, they strengthen their sense of self-worth. Overcoming the fear of rejection, often rooted in a desire for approval, shifts the mindset from people-pleasing to self-respect. This assertiveness, when practiced consistently, earns respect from others and enhances one's ability to make confident, mindful decisions.

Mindfulness plays a critical role in saying no effectively.

By pausing before responding, identifying emotional triggers, and reflecting on alignment with core values, individuals can ensure their decisions are intentional rather than impulsive. Practicing mindful communication allows them to decline gracefully without alienating others. Self-compassion, another key aspect of mindfulness, helps mitigate feelings of guilt when saying no, reinforcing the validity of one's needs and values. Ultimately, embracing 'no' leads to personal growth by fostering clarity, confidence, and purpose.

Whether it's a professional seeking balance, a social butterfly learning to prioritize downtime, or an entrepreneur focusing on core goals, 'no' transforms chaotic lives into intentional ones.

As spiritual teachings and life experiences show, saying no is not just a refusal, it is a profound affirmation of self, enabling a life of authenticity, fulfilment, and resilience.

9

Cultural and Societal Perspectives on Saying No

Saying no is the first step to a meaningful yes.
Only by refusing the unnecessary can you
embrace the essential.

—Osho, The Book of Secrets

Saying no is a fundamental aspect of human communication, yet its cultural and societal implications vary widely.

Across the globe, the act of refusal is deeply intertwined with notions of politeness, respect, hierarchy, and individualism. Some societies view 'no' as a powerful assertion of personal boundaries, while others consider it a disruption of harmony or a challenge to social norms.

Let us talk about the cultural and societal perspectives on saying no—shedding light on its complexities, nuances, and the consequences of its use or avoidance.

Saying no can evoke feelings of guilt, fear, or liberation, depending on the context. For many, 'no' represents the assertion of boundaries and the rejection of undue obligations. However, in numerous cultures, this straightforward response is often shrouded in layers of euphemism and indirectness.

In Western cultures, especially in countries like the United States, saying no is often celebrated as an act of personal empowerment. In contrast, collectivist cultures, such as those in Japan or India, often prioritize social harmony over individual assertiveness, making direct refusals more nuanced and indirect.

In individualistic societies, such as those in North America and parts of Europe, assertiveness is frequently viewed as a positive trait. Refusing an unreasonable request is seen as a sign of self-respect and independence. From early childhood, individuals in these cultures are encouraged to express their preferences, even if it means contradicting others.

For example, in the United States the phrase 'just say no' became a cultural catchphrase during the 1980s as part of a campaign against drug use. This slogan epitomized the belief that personal discretion and the ability to refuse were integral to individual success and societal well-being.

However, this emphasis on assertiveness can sometimes lead to friction in multicultural interactions, where differing norms around refusal might create misunderstandings.

In collectivist cultures, such as Japan, India, and much of Southeast Asia, saying no directly is often avoided to preserve harmony and maintain relationships.

Refusals are typically wrapped in ambiguity or softened through alternative expressions. For instance, a Japanese individual might say, '*chotto muzukashii*' (literally 'it's a bit difficult') instead of outright rejecting a request. This phrase allows the speaker to convey reluctance without causing offense or embarrassment to the other party. An Indian may say '*sochte hain*' (literally, 'let me think') instead of saying no. In both instances, the intention could be a soft way to communicate a no!

In my early years in Singapore, I often experienced asking a business associate from Southeast Asia or China for something related to work when they replied with phrases like 'I will think about it' or 'I will check and revert,' I interpreted their responses as genuine interest. Only later did I realize these were polite ways of declining, illustrating the challenges of navigating cultural subtleties in communication.

Ramesh, a 28-year-old IT professional from Chennai, was approached by his elder cousin with a business proposal. While Ramesh didn't find the proposal viable, he knew that a direct no might harm their relationship. Instead of outright refusing, he said, 'This sounds interesting, but I'll need time to consider it.' Over the next few days, Ramesh subtly steered the conversation toward other possibilities without directly declining. His careful handling of the situation helped him avoid conflict while preserving familial respect.

In many Middle Eastern and African cultures, community and relationships often take precedence over individual preference. Refusing a request outright may be perceived as a lack of generosity or hospitality. Instead, refusals are often couched in elaborate expressions of regret.

'He alone is a conqueror, who conquers his mind,'[45] says the Guru Granth Sahib ji.

A fascinating example comes from Senegal, where the concept of *Teranga*, literally means a value that encompasses hospitality, respect, community, and solidarity. It's a way of treating guests with open arms and a seat around the table

[45]Guru Granth Sahib, Ang 1186.

making it challenging to say no. If a neighbour asks for help, it is almost unthinkable to refuse outright, even if it means stretching one's resources.

Similarly, in Arab cultures, the phrase '*Insha Allah*' (God willing) is sometimes used as a way to delay or softly decline a commitment without offending the requester.

In many societies, the act of refusal intersects with gender expectations, adding another layer of complexity. Women, in particular, often face greater societal pressure to comply with requests due to traditional roles as caregivers and nurturers.

In Western feminist discourse, the ability to say no is often framed as a crucial element of empowerment. Campaigns such as 'No Means No', which address consent and sexual autonomy, highlight the societal importance of respecting boundaries. The movement emphasizes that 'No' is a complete sentence, requiring neither justification nor elaboration.

In more patriarchal societies, saying no can carry significant consequences, particularly for women. In some traditional communities, women who refuse to comply with societal expectations may face ostracization or worse.

A striking anecdote involves Malala Yousafzai, who famously defied the Taliban's ban on girls' education in Pakistan. Her refusal to comply with oppressive norms highlights the profound impact of saying no in challenging unjust systems. Her courage underscores the transformative potential of refusal when used to uphold fundamental rights.

Priya, a homemaker from a small village in Rajasthan, often found herself burdened by expectations from extended family members who would call on her for additional help during gatherings. For years, she felt obligated to comply, but it drained her physically and emotionally. One day, when her sister-in-law asked for help preparing a large meal, Priya said, 'I'm happy to help, but I'll only be able to assist for an hour.' This small but firm refusal was a turning point in her life, helping her set boundaries and gain respect within the family.

The workplace presents unique challenges in navigating refusals, as professional relationships often hinge on diplomacy and collaboration. In hierarchical cultures, such as those in India or South Korea, subordinates may find it particularly difficult to say no to superiors, fearing repercussions or being labelled as uncooperative.

In Western corporate environments, setting boundaries is increasingly recognized as essential to prevent burnout and maintain productivity. The advent of remote work has further emphasized the need for professionals to decline unreasonable demands on their time. Phrases like 'I don't have capacity for this right now' or 'Let me redirect you to someone who can help' have become part of the corporate lexicon.

In French culture, it is acceptable to say no directly but with finesse. A French colleague might say, 'No, I cannot, because I have other commitments,' emphasizing their rationale. Assertive communication balanced with justification is valued.

A German professional might say, 'No, this doesn't align with our priorities,' offering a clear explanation. This reflects their cultural emphasis on precision and order. Clarity and transparency are important when declining.

A Scandinavian individual might say no simply, 'No, I can't,' without further elaboration, reflecting a culture of honesty and minimalism. Directness and simplicity are appreciated.

Russians are often straightforward. A Russian businessperson might respond, 'No, this doesn't work for us,' reflecting their practicality. Honesty, even if blunt, is respected.

In contrast, Asian workplaces often require employees to employ indirect language when declining requests.

In South Korea or India, a junior employee might say, 'I'll try my best' as a way of signalling that a task may not be feasible. Such nuanced communication reflects a broader cultural emphasis on respect and deference within professional hierarchies. 'Before you say yes to others, make sure you are not saying no to yourself,'[46] says Acharya Chanakya.

A Chinese businessperson might say, 'Let's discuss this later,' as a polite way of rejecting a deal. This helps maintain harmony without direct refusal. Therefore, preserving relationships is key when saying no.

Saying no in Arab cultures might involve soft refusals like, 'Insha Allah' (God willing), implying no without directly stating it. For example, a host might agree to a guest's request but subtly indicate it's inconvenient.

In many African cultures, saying no might involve a story or parable to explain the refusal, such as, 'The hunter does not chase two hares at once.' This softens the impact of the refusal. Cultural wisdom often underpins refusals.

From a psychological perspective, the ability to say no is closely tied to self-esteem and emotional well-being.

---

[46]Chanakya Neeti, Chapter 8.

Research indicates that people who struggle to refuse requests often experience higher levels of stress and resentment. Conversely, those who assert their boundaries tend to report greater satisfaction and autonomy.

Saying no is not merely an act of refusal; it is a profound expression of agency, values, and identity. While cultural and societal norms shape how refusals are communicated, the underlying importance of boundaries and autonomy remains universal. Whether it is a Japanese businessman softening his refusal with ambiguity, a feminist reclaiming her right to reject, or an activist defying injustice, the word no carries immense power.

Meera, a young woman from a conservative family in Uttar Pradesh, was expected to study medicine, following the path set by her elder siblings. However, her passion lay in art and design. When she informed her parents of her decision to pursue a creative career, they were shocked. Despite their initial resistance, Meera stood firm and explained, 'I respect your wishes, but I want to explore a field where I feel truly inspired.' Eventually, her persistence paid off, and she went on to win a national award for her work. Meera's courage to say no to societal norms became a source of inspiration for many girls in her town.

By understanding the cultural and societal dimensions of saying no, we can foster greater empathy and adaptability in our interactions. Ultimately, the ability to say no with clarity and respect is a skill that transcends borders, enabling individuals to navigate their lives with integrity and purpose.

As the old adage goes, 'A strong yes requires a strong no.'

10

Understanding How Saying No Can Lead to Better Choices

Learn to say no to the good so you can say yes to the best.

—John C. Maxwell

The simple act of saying no holds an immense power that many people struggle to harness. From childhood, we are often encouraged to say yes. We say yes to opportunities, to others' requests, and even to ideas that do not serve us well.

However, the ability to say no is just as important, if not more so, because it enables us to set boundaries, focus on what truly matters, and make better decisions. Saying no is a key skill for living a fulfilled and balanced life. It protects our time, energy, and mental space and helps us remain aligned with our values and long-term goals.

The Difficulty of Saying No

Saying no is often uncomfortable for many reasons. Psychologically, humans are social creatures, and we are wired to seek acceptance and avoid conflict. Saying no can create a sense of rejection. Whether we are rejecting others' expectations or perceived opportunities, most of us find it difficult to say no.

According to social psychologist Roy Baumeister[47], we are motivated by a 'need to belong', and rejection can trigger feelings of anxiety or guilt. This discomfort can drive people to agree to things they don't want to do, leading to unnecessary commitments and eventual burnout.

Moreover, the fear of missing out has become more prevalent in the modern world. Social media amplifies this anxiety, with people constantly exposed to curated images of others enjoying various opportunities. The pressure to say yes and stay involved is high, especaiIly when those activities do not align with one's values or interests.

As psychologist Susan Newman[48] notes, 'The fear of missing out can push us to say yes when, in fact, we are sacrificing our own needs and desires.' Understanding this pressure is the first step toward making more mindful choices by learning when and how to say no.

The Power of Boundaries

One of the most important benefits of saying no is the establishment of boundaries. Setting clear personal boundaries allows us to protect our time, energy, and

---

[47]Baumeister, Roy F., and Mark R. Leary. 'The Need to Belong: Desire for Interpersonal Attachments as a Fundamental Human Motivation.' Psychological Bulletin, vol. 117, no. 3, 1995, pp. 497–529.
[48]Newman, Susan. The Book of No: 365 Ways to Say It and Mean It—and Stop People-Pleasing Forever. TarcherPerigee, 2017.

mental well-being. Brené Brown[49], a researcher and author on vulnerability and courage, explains that boundaries are crucial to leading a compassionate life: 'Daring to set boundaries is about having the courage to love ourselves even when we risk disappointing others.' By saying no to things that violate our boundaries, we demonstrate respect for ourselves and our priorities.

Priya was a hardworking employee who wanted to be seen as reliable. Her manager approached her with a new project, but Priya knew that her current tasks were already demanding. Despite initial hesitation, she politely explained her workload and said, 'I would love to help, but I won't be able to give my best with my current commitments.' Her manager respected her decision and reassigned the project. This incident taught Priya that setting boundaries by saying no not only helps maintain productivity but also fosters respect and trust at work.

Boundaries also prevent us from overextending ourselves. In today's fast-paced world, many people feel overwhelmed by the sheer number of obligations and responsibilities they face. Saying yes too often can lead to a life where we are constantly reacting to external demands rather than proactively shaping our own path. By saying no to trivial tasks and distractions, we create space to focus on what truly matters.

---

[49]Brown, Brené. *Daring Greatly: How the Courage to Be Vulnerable Transforms the Way We Live, Love, Parent, and Lead.* Avery, 2015.

Protecting Time and Energy

One of the most tangible advantages of saying no is that it allows us to protect our time and energy, two finite resources that are often spread too thin. When we say yes to every request, we deplete our energy on tasks that may not align with our priorities.

Time management expert Laura Vanderkam[50] emphasizes the importance of intentional time use in her book *168 Hours: You Have More Time Than You Think.* She writes, 'If you don't determine how your time is best spent, other people will determine it for you.' By learning to say no we take control of our schedule and invest our time in activities that provide meaning and fulfilment.

Saying no also enhances our productivity.

Aarav often felt drained because he always said yes to his friends' weekend plans, afraid they might feel hurt if he refused. As a result, he rarely got time to recharge. One Friday evening, he decided to politely say, 'I really need some time for myself this weekend.' Instead of feeling guilty, he used the time to rest, read a book, and go for a quiet walk. He felt rejuvenated and realized that saying no allowed him to invest in self-care. Aarav's experience highlights how protecting our time by saying no leads to better energy and well-being.

In today's world of constant notifications and demands for attention, focus is often elusive. Cal Newport[51], author of *Deep Work: Rules for Focused Success in a Distracted World,*

---

[50]Vanderkam, Laura. *168 Hours: You Have More Time Than You Think.* Portfolio, 2010.

[51]Newport, Cal. *Deep Work: Rules for Focused Success in a Distracted World.* Grand Central Publishing, 2016.

emphasizes the importance of deep, undistracted work to produce valuable results. He argues that achieving excellence in any field requires concentrated time and energy, which is only possible when distractions are minimized. Saying no to unnecessary meetings, emails, and trivial commitments allows us to carve out time for deep work and creative thinking, leading to better outcomes.

Aligning with Personal Values

Another key aspect of saying no is that it allows us to stay aligned with our personal values and long-term goals. When we say yes to everything, we dilute our focus and may find ourselves pursuing goals that do not resonate with our core beliefs.

Saying no to distractions and opportunities that do not align with our values also fosters a greater sense of purpose. When we focus on what truly matters to us, we experience greater fulfilment and meaning in our lives.

Meera had always been passionate about photography, but her schedule was filled with tasks and favours for others. She rarely had time for her hobby. One day, she decided to start saying no to nonessential commitments. This freed up her evenings and weekends, which she dedicated to photography. Soon, she began sharing her photos online, and her work was featured in a local exhibition. Meera realized that saying no to distractions allowed her to align her life with her true passion and long-term goals.

Research on motivation has shown that intrinsic motivation leads to greater well-being than extrinsic motivation, which is driven by external rewards. By saying no to things that do not resonate with our intrinsic motivations, we create space for activities that bring genuine joy and satisfaction.

Making Better Decisions

Saying no also leads to better decision-making.

In his book *The Paradox of Choice: Why More is Less*, psychologist Barry Schwartz[52] argues that having too many options can lead to decision fatigue and paralysis. When we feel obligated to say yes to everything, we overwhelm ourselves with too many choices, making it harder to prioritize effectively. On the other hand, learning to say no allows us to focus on fewer, higher-quality options, leading to more thoughtful and deliberate decisions.

Kabir's friends often invited him to join their study groups. Although he wanted to focus on solo studying, he always said yes fearing he'd miss out on something. Eventually, he noticed his grades slipping. He decided to say no to group sessions and focused on his personal study plan. His grades improved, and he felt more confident about his preparation. This experience taught Kabir that saying no helped him make better academic decisions and prioritize activities that genuinely contributed to his success.

Developing Confidence and Self-Respect

Learning to say no not only leads to better external outcomes but also fosters greater confidence and self-respect. Many

---

[52]Schwartz, Barry. *The Paradox of Choice: Why More Is Less.* Harper Perennial, 2004.

people struggle with self-worth and feel that they need to say yes to gain approval or validation from others. However, constantly seeking approval from others can lead to resentment and dissatisfaction, as we neglect our own needs in favour of others' expectations. The greatest gift we can give ourselves is the gift of self-love and self-respect.

When we learn to say no, we develop a stronger sense of self-worth and assert our right to prioritize our own well-being. Saying no is a form of self-care, as it allows us to create boundaries and protect ourselves from unnecessary stress and exhaustion. Over time, this practice builds confidence, as we learn to trust our instincts and make decisions that are in our best interest.

Avoiding Burnout

In our increasingly busy and demanding world, burnout is a growing concern. Ananya was known for her dedication at work. Because she rarely said no to additional tasks, she often stayed late and skipped personal time. Eventually, she started feeling exhausted and less enthusiastic about her job. One day, she mustered the courage to say no to an extra assignment, explaining that she needed to maintain a balance. Her boss appreciated her honesty and reassigned the task. Ananya felt relieved and more energized. This incident showed her that saying no helped prevent burnout and kept her motivated.

The World Health Organization has officially recognized burnout as a workplace phenomenon characterized by chronic stress, fatigue, and a lack of accomplishment. One of the key factors contributing to burnout is the inability to say no to excessive demands. When we take on too much, we stretch ourselves too thin and risk losing our passion and motivation.

Saying no is an essential tool for preventing burnout. By setting limits on our time and energy, we ensure that we have the resources to recharge and maintain our well-being. Saying no to over commitment allows us to maintain a healthy balance between work, personal life, and self-care, leading to greater long-term success and fulfilment.

Practical Strategies for Saying No

Despite the benefits of saying no, many people struggle to do so in practice. The fear of disappointing others or missing out can be overwhelming. However, there are practical strategies that can make saying no easier and more effective.

One strategy is to delay your response. If we are unsure whether to commit to something, it is okay to take time to think it over. By giving ourselves space to evaluate the request, we can make a more informed decision without feeling pressured to say yes in the moment. We might say, 'Let me check my schedule and get back to you' or 'I need to think about that and will let you know.'

Another approach is to be polite but firm. We do not need to offer a lengthy explanation or apology when we say no. A simple, direct response such as 'Thank you for the offer, but I'm unable to commit at this time' is enough. By being clear and respectful, we maintain our boundaries while still showing consideration for the other person.

It's also important to remember that saying no is not the same as being selfish.

In fact, saying no can make us more effective and reliable in the long run, as we are able to focus on the commitments that truly matter.

▪

Saying no is a powerful but often difficult skill to master. Many of us are taught from a young age to say yes to opportunities, requests, and ideas. While saying yes can open doors, learning when to say no is just as important because it helps us focus on what truly matters and make better choices.

Saying no feels hard for many reasons. We want to be liked, avoid conflict, and fear missing out on things that seem exciting or important. Social media adds to this fear, showing us the best moments from other people's lives, which makes us feel pressure to stay involved in everything. This often results in saying yes too often, which can leave us feeling overwhelmed and stretched too thin.

One of the biggest benefits of saying no is that it helps set healthy boundaries. Boundaries protect our time, energy, and mental well-being. Brené Brown, a researcher on human behaviour, explains that setting boundaries is key to self-respect. When we say no to things that don't serve us, we show respect for ourselves and our priorities.

By saying no more often, we can focus better on what really matters. Time and energy are limited, so we must be wise in how we use them. If we say yes to too many things, we end up losing time for tasks and people that are most important to us. Time expert Laura Vanderkam says that if we don't take control of how we spend our time, others will do it for us. Saying no allows us to choose how we want to use our time wisely.

Saying no also helps us stay true to our values. When we say yes to things that don't match our goals, we risk losing focus. But if we say no to unimportant tasks, we have more time to do what matters, which makes us feel happier and more fulfilled. Psychologists say that having fewer but more meaningful choices improves decision-making and reduces stress.

Learning to say no builds confidence. Many people feel they need to say yes to be accepted, but always agreeing with others can lead to stress and unhappiness. Saying no is a way to care for yourself and protect your energy. Over time, it helps you feel stronger and more in control of your life.

In a busy world, saying no can prevent burnout. When we set limits on what we take on, we keep a healthy balance in life. Simple strategies, like pausing before giving an answer or politely declining, can make saying no easier.

Learning to say no leads to better choices and a more balanced, happy life.

11

The Power of Saying No—Understanding Rejection, Approval, and Guilt

The power to say no is one of the most transformative tools in human interaction. It is not merely an act of rejection but a boundary-setting mechanism, a declaration of self-respect, and a vital tool for personal and spiritual growth. Saying no can be a daunting task, often intertwined with feelings of guilt, fear of rejection, and the desire for approval. However, understanding the deeper implications of saying no allows one to harness its power positively.

Lessons from our scriptures offer profound insights into the nuances of rejection, approval, and guilt, demonstrating that saying no is not only permissible but often essential for a balanced and purposeful life.

In the Bible, Jesus exemplifies the power of saying no in his interactions with the Pharisees and during his time of temptation in the wilderness. When Satan tempts him with offers of worldly power, glory, and material comfort, Jesus firmly rejects these temptations, saying no to what would divert him from his divine mission[53]. His refusal is a testament to unwavering commitment to his higher purpose.

Guru Nanak Dev Ji's rejection of material wealth is a profound lesson in detachment. When Malik Bhago, a wealthy man, offered him a feast made from ill-gotten wealth, Guru Nanak refused and instead ate from the humble offering of Bhai Lalo, a poor carpenter. He demonstrated that saying no to what is morally wrong empowers one to live a righteous life.

'As Gurmukh, look upon pleasure and pain as one and the same; eradicate selfishness and conceit from within.'[54]

Jesus often challenged societal norms and expectations, rejecting hypocrisy and superficial religiosity. In Luke 11:37–54, he openly criticizes the Pharisees, saying no to their oppressive interpretations of the law. His actions demonstrate that saying no is not about defiance for its own sake but about courageously upholding truth and authenticity.

Guilt often accompanies the act of saying no, especially in cultures that prioritize collective harmony over individual needs.

The Mahabharata illustrates this through the story of Karna, a loyal friend to Duryodhana. Despite knowing that Duryodhana's cause is unjust, Karna cannot say no to him because of a sense of loyalty and fear of rejection. His inability to refuse leads to his tragic downfall, teaching us that saying yes at the cost of our principles can have far-reaching consequences.

The Bible also addresses guilt and the desire for approval

---

[53]The Bible, Matthew 4:1–11.

[54]Guru Granth Sahib, Ang 219.

through the story of Martha and Mary[55]. When Jesus visits their home, Martha busies herself with preparations while Mary sits at his feet, listening to him. Martha, seeking approval for her efforts, complains that Mary is not helping her. Jesus gently rebukes Martha, affirming that Mary has chosen the better path by prioritizing spiritual nourishment over societal expectations. This episode reminds us that saying no to unnecessary obligations allows us to focus on what truly matters.

Saying no does not mean rejecting people or relationships; rather, it is a way to establish healthy boundaries.

In the Ramayana, Lord Rama exemplifies this balance. When Queen Kaikeyi demands that he leave the kingdom and live in exile for 14 years, Rama accepts her command. He does not harbour resentment or guilt but instead views the situation as part of his dharma. Rama's response demonstrates that rejection, when accompanied by compassion and understanding, can preserve relationships while maintaining integrity.

In the New Testament, Jesus balances rejection with compassion when he tells his disciples to 'shake the dust off their feet[56]' if a town does not welcome them. This act symbolizes the importance of moving on without bitterness or guilt when faced with rejection, ensuring emotional well-being and focus on their mission.

A man once insulted the Buddha but instead of reacting the Buddha asked, 'If someone offers you a gift and you refuse to accept it, to whom does it belong?' The man answered,

---

[55]Bible, Luke 10:38–42.

[56]Bible, Matthew 10:14.

'To the one who offered it.' The Buddha explained that by saying no to anger and resentment, one can free themselves from emotional suffering.

'He insulted me, he struck me, he defeated me, he robbed me—in those who harbour such thoughts, hatred will never cease.'[57]

The lessons from these scriptures hold immense relevance today. In a world that often equates busyness with worth and agreement with harmony, saying no is an act of self-preservation. It enables individuals to prioritize their mental and emotional well-being, focus on their goals, and stay true to their values.

For instance, a professional who constantly agrees to additional responsibilities out of fear of rejection may face burnout and diminished productivity. By learning to say no with grace and confidence, they can manage their workload effectively and maintain balance. Similarly, in personal relationships, saying no to toxic behaviours or unreasonable demands fosters healthier interactions and mutual respect.

The power of saying no lies in its ability to affirm one's values, set boundaries, and prioritize what truly matters. Insights from the Bhagavad Gita, the Bible, and other spiritual texts remind us that saying no is not an act of selfishness but one of self-respect and moral clarity. Whether it is rejecting distractions, standing firm against societal pressures, or overcoming guilt, the act of saying no is a transformative step toward personal growth and spiritual fulfilment.

By embracing the power of saying no, we can navigate the complexities of rejection, approval, and guilt with

---

[57]Dhammapada, Verse 3.

wisdom and compassion, ultimately leading lives of greater authenticity and purpose.

Noted psychologist Carl Rogers, in his book *On Becoming a Person*, explores the deep need for positive regard from others, which often leads to a fear of rejection. He writes, 'The degree to which I can be open to the experience of being disliked, judged, or rejected is the degree to which I will be free from the fear of rejection.' (Rogers, 1961). The key to overcoming the fear of rejection lies in cultivating the ability to accept that rejection is a part of life and that it does not diminish one's inherent worth.

Saying yes to every request out of a desire to be liked or admired can lead to burnout, resentment, and even a loss of personal identity. Brené Brown, in her book *The Gifts of Imperfection*, explains that the search for approval can be toxic, writing, 'When we focus on pleasing others, we lose our sense of worthiness.' Her work encourages individuals to prioritize self-compassion and authenticity over external validation.

The pervasive nature of social media and constant digital connectivity has exacerbated this need for approval. Individuals are bombarded with likes, comments, and shares, which can create a false sense of validation. Saying no in this context becomes even harder, as the fear of missing out on opportunities for approval becomes a driving force in decision-making.

The Sikh Gurus often faced rejection and persecution for their teachings. Yet, they rejected the need for worldly approval, focusing instead on their duty to uphold truth and justice. Guru Arjan Dev Ji's martyrdom exemplifies how saying no to injustice and standing firm in spiritual conviction requires immense strength.

'Why should I be afraid? The Lord Himself is my protector. By His Grace, I have dispelled all fear.'[58]

Simon Sinek in *Leaders Eat Last* argues that the constant need for social affirmation can undermine our ability to make authentic decisions, saying, 'We are designed to need others, but that also makes us vulnerable to their opinions.' He advocates for developing stronger boundaries and understanding that real approval comes from within, not from external sources.

Religious scriptures have also addressed the issue of approval. In the Bible Jesus advises against seeking approval from others in his Sermon on the Mount:

'Beware of practicing your righteousness before other people in order to be seen by them, for then you will have no reward from your Father who is in heaven.'[59]

This teaching underscores the idea that seeking approval from others is fleeting and that true fulfilment comes from living in alignment with one's values and principles. Ultimately, the danger of seeking approval is that it leads to decision-making that is not aligned with one's true self. Learning to say no is an act of reclaiming personal agency and living authentically, regardless of external validation.

Saying no to people, even those we love can be one of the most courageous and necessary acts we perform. But the guilt that comes with it can be overwhelming. We must recognize that guilt is a natural emotion but should not dictate one's actions.

---

[58]Guru Granth Sahib, Ang 819.

[59]Bible, Matthew 6:1.

A useful framework for overcoming guilt can be found in Stoic philosophy. The Stoics taught that guilt, like all emotions, is a result of our judgments rather than external events. Epictetus, in his *Discourses,* writes, 'No one can make you feel guilty without your consent'[60]. This suggests that guilt is a choice and that by changing our perspective on saying no, we can eliminate the unnecessary guilt that accompanies it.

Saying no is an important skill that helps people take care of themselves, set clear limits, and stay true to their values. However, many find it hard to say no because they fear being rejected, want others to approve of them, or feel guilty. By understanding why these feelings arise and learning how to manage them, people can build the confidence to say no when they need to.

Overcoming the fear of rejection requires accepting that rejection is a normal part of life and does not diminish one's worth. Addressing the need for approval involves cultivating self-worth from within rather than seeking validation from others. Finally, managing guilt requires recognizing that saying no is not an act of selfishness but an act of self-care that benefits both the individual and those around them.

By mastering the art of saying no, individuals can make decisions that align with their values, and live more fulfilling, authentic lives.

The following passage from Ayn Rand's *Fountainhead*[61] explains this thought brilliantly:

---

[60]While commonly attributed to Epictetus, the exact wording of this quote is not found in his surviving works. It reflects the Stoic philosophy articulated in texts like *The Enchiridion* and *Discourses.*

[61]Rand, Ayn. *The Fountainhead.* Bobbs-Merrill, 1943.

'Do you mean to tell me that you're thinking seriously of building that way, when and if you are an architect?'

'Yes.'

'My dear fellow, who will let you?'

'That's not the point. The point is, who will stop me?'

Angulimala, a notorious bandit who repented and became a disciple of the Buddha, initially struggled with guilt over his past. Buddha taught him that saying no to self-condemnation and focusing on the present moment leads to liberation. Angulimala's transformation underscores the power of rejecting guilt to embrace spiritual growth.

'You yourself must strive. The Buddhas only point the way.'[62]

The power to say no is, ultimately, the power to shape one's own life.

▪

The ability to say no is a transformative skill in life and work.

While it may seem like an act of rejection, it is fundamentally about setting boundaries, maintaining self-respect, and fostering personal growth. Saying no is difficult due to emotional hurdles like guilt, fear of rejection, and the desire for approval. However, by understanding its deeper significance, we can use it as a tool for balance and purpose.

Lessons from religious texts highlight the importance of saying no in alignment with personal values. In the Bible, Jesus repeatedly said no to temptations that could divert him from his spiritual mission, illustrating how refusal can strengthen commitment to higher goals. Similarly, Guru

---

[62]Dhammapada, Verse 276.

Nanak Dev Ji's rejection of ill-gotten wealth teaches us to stand firm in moral integrity.

Fear of rejection is a common reason people avoid saying no. Stories from the Mahabharata, such as Karna's tragic loyalty to Duryodhana, reveal how saying yes against one's better judgment can lead to undesirable consequences. This highlights the need to prioritize principles over the fear of displeasing others.

Many cultures emphasize harmony, making refusal uncomfortable and often accompanied by guilt. The story of Martha and Mary in the Bible shows how Martha's desire for approval led to misplaced priorities. Jesus' response emphasizes the importance of focusing on what truly matters; reminding us that saying no to unnecessary obligations enables us to pursue meaningful goals.

At work, professionals often say yes to every request, fearing rejection or missing opportunities. This can result in burnout and reduced effectiveness. Learning to say no allows individuals to manage their responsibilities better and maintain a healthy work-life balance. Similarly, in personal life, saying no to toxic relationships or unreasonable demands fosters mutual respect and emotional well-being.

Saying no with compassion is equally important. Lord Rama's response to Queen Kaikeyi's demand for exile in the Ramayana shows how rejection, when handled gracefully, can preserve relationships while maintaining integrity. Similarly, Jesus advised his disciples to move on peacefully when faced with rejection, symbolizing emotional detachment without resentment.

Philosophers and psychologists also emphasize the importance of mastering the art of refusal. Carl Rogers discusses how freeing oneself from the fear of rejection is essential for personal growth. Brené Brown warns that excessive approval-seeking erodes authenticity and self-worth.

Social media amplifies the pressure to seek external validation, making it harder to say no. Yet, the key to authenticity lies in setting clear boundaries, as Simon Sinek suggests in *Leaders Eat Last.* True fulfilment comes from living by one's values, not by others' expectations.

Overcoming guilt is crucial in adopting this practice. Stoic philosophy teaches that emotions like guilt are rooted in perception, and by reframing our mindset, we can refuse unnecessary guilt. Angulimala's story in Buddhist teachings shows how rejecting self-condemnation fosters spiritual liberation.

Ultimately, saying no is about reclaiming personal agency. By doing so, we prioritize our well-being, strengthen relationships, and lead purposeful, authentic lives.

12

Challenges We Face in Accepting No for an Answer

He who sees all beings in his own Self,
and his own Self in all beings, does not
feel rejected by anyone.

—Isha Upanishad, Verse 6

In life, we often want things to go our way. A 'yes' often brings comfort, but a 'no' can evoke resistance, disappointment, or even resentment. Whether it is at home, at work, or in society, hearing a 'yes' makes us feel good. It means we are accepted, our ideas are approved, and we get what we want. However, when we hear a 'no', it brings disappointment. It can feel like rejection, criticism, or even failure. This reaction is natural because, as human beings, we don't like being turned down.

The Upanishads emphasize oneness with the universe. When we internalize that rejection is not personal but part of the collective experience, we cultivate resilience. This perspective can be particularly helpful in societal contexts where rejection might stem from prejudice or misunderstanding. Developing inner strength allows us to navigate rejection with empathy rather than bitterness.

Yet, learning how to handle a 'no' is a crucial life skill. It helps us grow stronger, become more resilient, and manage relationships better.

Sant Kabir stated, 'Kabira, when ego dies, only then does the soul awaken.'

Kabir's teachings highlight that ego is the root of suffering when faced with rejection. Whether at home, or in social settings, a 'no' often bruises our ego. By letting go of ego, we learn to accept rejection gracefully and use it as a means of personal growth. This perspective fosters humility, improving our relationships with family and society.

Hearing no can have a significant impact on our ego, often triggering feelings of rejection, inadequacy, or self-doubt.

The ego, which thrives on validation and affirmation, perceives 'no' as a threat to its self-image and sense of worth. This response stems from the fear of failure or being perceived as less capable by others. While initially painful, hearing no can also foster resilience and personal growth by challenging the ego's need for constant approval. By learning to detach our self-worth from external validation, we can develop greater emotional maturity, turning rejection into a stepping-stone for future success.

▪

Let us examine the challenges we face when hearing 'no', how it affects us emotionally and mentally, and ways to accept it gracefully. Let us also discuss specific situations where handling 'no' can be difficult, within families, at work, and in society.

Why We Struggle to Accept No

The difficulty in accepting 'no' often comes from our expectations. When we ask for something or express a desire, we naturally hope to receive a positive response. A 'yes' makes us feel valued and appreciated. On the other hand, a 'no' feels personal. It is difficult to accept and internalise. It can hurt our pride, challenge our sense of worth, and sometimes make us question our relationships.

'The moment you need others to agree with you, you become their prisoner.'[63]

Jiddu Krishnamurthy emphasizes the importance of inner freedom. At home, when parents reject a child's request, or in society when one's ideas are not accepted, seeking approval can lead to frustration. True liberation comes from self-acceptance and understanding that external validation is not essential for inner peace.

Emotional Reactions to Rejection

1. *Feeling of Rejection*: When we hear 'no', especially from someone close to us, it feels like they are rejecting us, not just our request. This can lead to feelings of sadness or even anger.
2. *Loss of Control*: A 'no' reminds us that we cannot always control everything. This loss of control can cause frustration.
3. *Fear of Failure*: Rejection can make us feel like we have failed. Whether it is a proposal at work or a

---

[63]Jiddu Krishnamurthy.

simple request at home, hearing 'no' might make us doubt our abilities.

4. *Ego Hurt*: Our ego often gets bruised when someone says 'no' to us. We may feel that our importance or authority has been diminished.

These reactions are common, but they do not have to define how we handle rejection.

'Adversity is the first path to truth.'[64] Vidura's wisdom in the Mahabharata highlights that rejection and failure offer valuable lessons. A 'no' at work, such as being passed over for a promotion, can be a stepping stone for personal development. Instead of resenting rejection, one should introspect and learn, thereby turning setbacks into opportunities for self-improvement.

With practice, we can learn to accept 'no' without feeling defeated.

Handling No at Home

Our home is where we feel safe and loved. However, it is also where we hear no most often. From our parents, spouse, or children. Accepting no at home can be particularly hard because it comes from people we care about the most.

1. *With Parents*: Parents often say no to protect us or guide us. As children, we may not understand this and feel upset. Even as adults, hearing no from parents can make us feel like we are still being treated as kids.

---

[64]Vidura Neeti, Mahabharata.

Parents often have more life experience and may see risks we don't. Trying to understand their reasons can make rejection easier to accept. Instead of reacting negatively, ask them why they said no. Open communication can lead to better understanding.

Even if we disagree with our parents' decision, it is important to stay respectful. Reacting calmly shows maturity.

2. *With a Spouse/Partner*: In a marriage or partnership, disagreements are common. Hearing no from a spouse can feel more personal because we expect our partner to support us. A 'no' can sometimes lead to arguments or hurt feelings.

   We must remember that we should not take a 'no' from our spouse or partner, personally. We must remember that a 'no' is about the situation and not a rejection of you as a person.

   Marriage is about give and take. If your spouse says no, try to find a middle ground where both of you can be happy. Timing matters. If you ask for something when your spouse is stressed or busy, they are more likely to say no.

3. *With Children*: As parents, we often say no to our children for their well-being. However, children may not always understand why we are rejecting their requests. This can lead to tantrums or rebellion.

   When saying no to children, explain why you have chosen to say no. This helps them learn and understand your decision. We need to be consistent in our responses. If we say no sometimes and yes other times for the same request, children get confused.

Being consistent helps them accept rejection better. Instead of just saying no, we could consider offering different options. For example, if a child wants to play video games late at night, we could suggest they play the next day instead.

Handling No in Society

In society, we face rejection in many forms. Whether it is being turned down for a job, not getting selected for a team, or having our ideas dismissed by a group. Such rejections can feel humiliating, especially when they happen publicly.

Some ways we can handle a 'no' in society could be:

1. *Stay Calm and Composed*: Public rejection can be embarrassing, but reacting angrily only makes things worse. Take a deep breath and stay calm.
2. *Learn from Rejection*: If your idea or application was rejected, ask for feedback. Use it as a learning opportunity to improve yourself.
3. *Build Resilience*: Remember that everyone faces rejection at some point. The key is to keep trying and not give up.

'With patience and faith, endure what comes your way, for by His will alone does the universe operate.'[65] The Sikh scripture teaches patience in the face of life's challenges. Rejection, whether in personal relationships or social settings, becomes manageable when we trust in a higher purpose. This perspective fosters patience and helps us endure 'no' without despair.

---

[65]Guru Granth Sahib, Ang 465.

Handling No at Work

At work, hearing no can be particularly challenging because it directly affects our career and professional growth. Whether it's a rejected project proposal, a denied promotion, or simply not being heard in a meeting, rejection at work can damage our confidence.

Here are some ways to handle a 'no' at work:

1. *Stay Professional*: Even if you feel hurt, it is important to remain professional. Avoid reacting emotionally in the workplace.
2. *Ask for Clarification*: If your proposal or request was rejected, ask your manager for the reasons behind their decision. This shows you are willing to learn and improve.
3. *Keep Improving*: Use rejection as motivation to do better. If you didn't get a promotion, work on your skills and try again next time.
4. *Support Others*: If a colleague faces rejection, support them. This creates a positive work environment where people feel valued, even when they hear no.

Turning No into a Positive Experience

While hearing a 'no' is never easy, it can be a positive experience if we approach it with the right mindset.

Here are some ways to turn rejection into an opportunity:

1. *Reframe Your Perspective*: Instead of seeing 'no' as a failure, see it as feedback. It is an opportunity to improve and grow.

2. *Practice Gratitude*: Even when rejected, be grateful for the chance to try. Each attempt teaches us something new.
3. *Stay Persistent*: Many successful people faced rejection before they succeeded. The key is to keep going and not give up.
4. *Focus on What You Can Control*: While you cannot control other people's responses, you can control how you react to them. Choose to respond positively.

'Ask, and it shall be given to you; seek, and ye shall find; knock, and it shall be opened unto you.'[66] This verse from The Bible encourages persistence in the face of no.

While a rejection may initially seem like a closed door, continuous effort and faith can lead to eventual success. Whether dealing with societal rejection or workplace denial, it's essential to stay hopeful, re-evaluate strategies, and continue moving forward. Accepting no as a temporary hurdle rather than a final barrier can help us grow.

▪

Learning to accept 'no' is an important part of life. Whether it comes from parents, a spouse, colleagues, or society, rejection is something everyone faces. While it may hurt initially, how we handle 'no' defines our character. By staying calm, seeking to understand the reasons behind the rejection, and using it as a learning experience, we can turn 'no' into a stepping stone toward success.

Noted poet Rumi has said, 'Try not to resist the changes

[66]Bible, Matthew Verse 7:7.

that come your way. Instead, let life live through you. And do not worry that your life is turning upside down. How do you know that the side you are used to is better than the one to come?'

Rumi's wisdom teaches that rejection is often life's way of redirecting us toward a better path. In social life, rejection by peers or groups can be painful, but embracing the possibility of a new direction helps transform the experience into an opportunity for new connections and personal growth.

Life is not about always hearing a 'yes'.

It is about how we handle the 'no' moments and continue to grow despite them. The sooner we accept that rejection is a natural part of life, the stronger and more resilient we will become.

▪

In life, hearing 'yes' is pleasing because it validates our ideas, choices, and worth.

Conversely, a 'no' can feel like rejection or failure, challenging our emotions and ego. We must understand why we struggle to accept 'no' and how learning to handle rejection helps us grow both personally and professionally.

The core issue behind our difficulty with rejection is expectation.

We naturally hope for positive responses, so when faced with a 'no', we often take it personally, leading to feelings of sadness, anger, or inadequacy. Jiddu Krishnamurthy's teaching on inner freedom reminds us that relying on others' approval can make us feel trapped. Accepting rejection with maturity allows us to maintain our peace of mind.

Emotional reactions to rejection are normal. Whether it's a bruised ego or frustration from losing control, these feelings can overwhelm us. However, great leaders and thinkers like Sant Kabir and Vidura remind us that adversity, including rejection, is a path to personal growth. With self-reflection, we can turn no into an opportunity to improve.

Rejections at home, whether from parents, a spouse, or children, are particularly tough because they come from people closest to us. Understanding the reasons behind a 'no' can foster open communication and empathy. For instance, when parents say no to protect us or guide us, their intention isn't to harm but to help. Similarly, handling a partner's no with respect and understanding builds stronger relationships. With children, consistent and clear communication about why we reject certain requests helps them learn to accept boundaries gracefully.

At work, rejection can affect our confidence and career growth. Whether it's a declined proposal or a missed promotion, hearing no can be disheartening. Staying professional, asking for feedback, and continually improving are key strategies to handle workplace rejections. Supporting colleagues who face rejection also fosters a positive work culture.

In society, rejection can come in various forms, such as being turned down for a job or having ideas dismissed. Public rejection may feel humiliating, but staying calm, seeking feedback, and building resilience helps us move forward.

We must develop the ability to reframe rejection into a stepping-stone rather than see it as a barrier. Learning to detach self-worth from external validation enables emotional maturity.

As Rumi wisely said, life's challenges can lead to unexpected growth. The ability to handle rejection with grace, introspection, and persistence is a skill that strengthens character and fosters success in both personal and professional spheres.

13

Overcoming Obstacles to No

Be the change you wish to see in the world.

—Mahatma Gandhi

The ability to say no is a vital skill that holds the power to transform our lives.

Yet, for many, it remains an elusive and challenging endeavour. Whether it stems from a desire to avoid conflict, a fear of disappointing others, or a deeply ingrained need for approval, saying no often feels like an insurmountable obstacle.

In this chapter let us explore the barriers that prevent us from embracing this simple yet powerful word.

Understanding the Fear behind No

The reluctance to say no is deeply rooted in our fears.

These fears take various forms, such as the fear of rejection, the fear of damaging relationships, and the fear of being perceived as selfish or unkind. These internal barriers are often shaped by societal expectations, cultural norms, and personal experiences.

1. *Fear of Rejection*: Many people equate saying no with the risk of alienation. This fear is particularly pronounced in professional settings, where declining requests might be seen as a lack of cooperation or ambition. Similarly, in personal relationships, the fear of rejection can compel individuals to say yes even when it comes at a personal cost.
   Ananya was a dedicated employee, always willing to stay late to help her team finish projects. But when her workload increased, she realized she couldn't manage everything. Yet, she feared that if she said no to her manager, he might think she wasn't committed enough. After overworking herself for weeks, she became exhausted. When she finally gathered the courage to say no, her manager surprised her by understanding and assigning another colleague to assist. Ananya learned that fear of rejection was mostly in her head.
2. *Fear of Conflict*: Some people avoid saying no to prevent potential confrontations. The assumption is that rejecting someone's request will lead to arguments, tension, or strained relationships. This fear often leads to people agreeing to things they neither want nor have the capacity to do.
   Arjun's friend frequently asked him for favours, like running errands or borrowing his car. Arjun didn't want to upset his friend, so he always said yes, even when it was inconvenient. Eventually, Arjun felt resentful. One day, he firmly but kindly said, 'I'm sorry, but I can't lend you my car this time.' To his surprise, his friend didn't get upset. He simply

found another way to manage. Arjun realized that the conflict he feared didn't even happen.

3. *Fear of Judgment*: Society often celebrates those who are endlessly accommodating and self-sacrificing. As a result, people worry that saying no will result in being judged as unkind, selfish, or uncooperative.
   Priya was part of a social group where everyone volunteered for different tasks. She always said yes to avoid being seen as unhelpful. One day, she couldn't take on a task because of work commitments. Nervously, she said, 'I won't be able to help this time.' Instead of judging her, her friends appreciated her honesty and reassured her that it was okay. Priya learned that people don't always judge as harshly as we imagine.
4. *Fear of Missed Opportunities*: There's also a pervasive fear of missing out (FOMO). Saying no might feel like closing the door on a potential opportunity, whether in personal growth, career advancement, or social connection.
   Rahul was an entrepreneur who said yes to every networking event and opportunity that came his way, hoping each would lead to something big. Eventually, he found himself overwhelmed and unable to focus on his core business. When he started saying no to events that didn't align with his goals, he had more time to focus on meaningful opportunities. This shift helped his business grow faster than before.

The Emotional Costs of Avoiding No

The inability to say no can lead to significant emotional and psychological strain. Constantly prioritizing others' needs over your own results in stress, burnout, and a diminished sense of self-worth. Over time, this pattern creates resentment, both toward those who make the requests and toward oneself for not establishing boundaries.

1. *Burnout*: Agreeing to every demand stretches your resources, time, energy, and emotional bandwidth, to the limit. The result is often chronic stress and exhaustion, which can lead to burnout.
   'Give, but give in such a way that your body, mind, and wealth are not exhausted.'[67]
   Nisha was a teacher who never declined extra responsibilities at school. Over time, she felt constantly tired and lost her enthusiasm for teaching. When she finally spoke to her principal and started saying no to some additional tasks, she felt more energized and could focus better on her students. Saying no helped her avoid burnout.
2. *Loss of Identity*: When you say yes too often, you may lose sight of your personal goals, values, and desires. This compromises your authenticity and can lead to a life that feels dictated by others rather than self-directed.
   Vikram loved painting, but after getting a job, he kept saying yes to every social invitation to avoid being seen as distant. Eventually, he realized he hadn't

---

[67]Guru Granth Sahib, Ang 1220.

painted in months, something that was once a big part of his life. When he started saying no to some social outings, he regained time for his passion and felt more like himself again.

3. *Erosion of Relationships*: Ironically, saying yes all the time can harm relationships. When people sense insincerity or detect hidden resentment, trust erodes, and relationships suffer.
   Meena always agreed to help her relatives, even when it was inconvenient. Over time, she felt taken for granted and grew resentful, which strained her relationships. When she started setting boundaries and saying no occasionally, her relationships improved because she was helping out of genuine willingness, not obligation.

Identifying the Root Causes of Resistance

To overcome the obstacles to no, it is essential to identify the root causes of resistance. These causes often stem from personal history, upbringing, and internalized beliefs.

1. *Cultural Conditioning*: In many cultures, compliance and self-sacrifice are viewed as virtues. People, especially women, are often raised to prioritize others' needs over their own. This conditioning reinforces the idea that saying no is inherently wrong.
   Amit grew up in a household where saying no was seen as disrespectful. Even as an adult, he found it difficult to decline requests, whether at work or with friends. It was not until a mentor pointed out that

setting boundaries is not about disrespect, but about mutual respect, that Amit started practicing saying no.

2. *Perfectionism and People-Pleasing*: Perfectionists often struggle with no because they feel the need to meet every expectation. Similarly, people-pleasers derive their sense of self-worth from making others happy, making 'no' feel like a threat to their identity. Neha always aimed to be the perfect employee, friend, and daughter. She felt guilty whenever she said no, thinking she was letting people down. One day, her manager told her, 'You don't have to be perfect at everything. Focus on what matters most.' This advice helped Neha realize that saying no to less important things allowed her to excel where it truly counted.
3. *Lack of Self-Awareness*: Sometimes, the inability to say no stems from not fully understanding one's own limits, values, or priorities. Without this clarity, it's easy to default to yes as a way to avoid introspection or difficult choices.
   Ravi often agreed to take on tasks because he wasn't clear about his own priorities. After a period of feeling overwhelmed, he began writing down his goals and limits. This exercise helped him understand when it was appropriate to say no. Over time, Ravi became more confident in his decisions.

Strategies for Overcoming the Obstacles to No

Now that we understand the barriers, how can we dismantle them? The following strategies offer a roadmap for reclaiming the power of no.

1. *Reframe Your Mindset*: Shift your perspective on 'no'. Instead of viewing it as a rejection, see it as an affirmation of your values and boundaries. Saying no is not about shutting people out but about creating space for what truly matters.
   Instead of seeing no as a rejection, Maya started viewing it as a way to prioritize her well-being. When her friend asked her to join a weekend trip, she said, 'No, I need some rest this weekend,' and spent her time recharging. Saying no felt empowering—not negative.
2. *Practice Self-Awareness*: Build a clear understanding of your priorities, values, and limits. Regular self-reflection, journaling, or working with a coach or therapist can help you gain clarity. Knowing what you stand for makes it easier to discern when to say no.
   Deepa started keeping a journal where she noted down situations where she said yes when she wanted to say no. Over time, she noticed patterns and became better at recognizing when to assert herself. This awareness helped her set healthier boundaries.
3. *Develop Assertiveness Skills*: Assertiveness is the ability to express your thoughts, feelings, and needs honestly and respectfully. Practice using 'I' statements, such as 'I feel overwhelmed when I take on too many commitments,' to communicate your boundaries without being confrontational.
   'Even if a snake is not poisonous, it should pretend to be venomous.'[68]

---

[68]Chanakya Neeti.

Manoj struggled with saying no politely but firmly. His coach taught him to use simple statements like, 'I can't take this on right now, but thank you for thinking of me.' Practicing these phrases in front of a mirror gave him the confidence to say no without feeling guilty.

4. *Start Small*: Begin by saying no in low-stakes situations to build confidence. For example, decline an invitation to a casual event or refuse a minor request at work. These small victories will empower you to handle more significant challenges.
   Rather than starting with a major no, Shruti began by declining small requests, like refusing a second helping of food when she wasn't hungry. These small acts of saying no built her confidence for bigger situations.
5. *Use the 'Positive No' Technique*: A 'Positive No' involves rejecting a request while offering an alternative or expressing appreciation. For instance, 'I can't take on this project right now, but I'd be happy to revisit it next month,' maintains goodwill while asserting your limits.
   When Raj's colleague asked him to help with a report, he said, 'I can't assist right now, but I can review it for you next week.' This way, Raj declined the immediate request while offering a helpful alternative. His colleague appreciated his honesty and support.
6. *Practice Self-Compassion*: Remind yourself that saying no doesn't make you a bad person. Be kind to yourself and understand that your well-being is just as important as anyone else's.

'Be kind to all beings; this is more meritorious than all worship and offerings.'[69]

Ayesha often felt guilty after saying no. Her therapist advised her to practice self-compassion by reminding herself, 'I deserve to take care of myself too.' Over time, this reduced her guilt and made saying no easier.

7. *Learn to Tolerate Discomfort*: Saying no might initially feel uncomfortable, especially if you're not used to it. Embrace this discomfort as part of the growth process. With practice, it will become easier and more natural.

   'The non-permanent appearance of happiness and distress, and their disappearance in due course, are like the appearance and disappearance of winter and summer seasons. They arise from sense perception, and one must learn to tolerate them without being disturbed.'[70]

   When Rohan first started saying no, he felt anxious and uncomfortable. But instead of giving up, he reminded himself that discomfort was temporary. Each time he said no it became a little easier, and soon he felt more at ease.

8. *Seek Support*: Surround yourself with people who respect and support your boundaries. Share your journey with trusted friends, family, or mentors who can provide encouragement and accountability.

   Pooja found it easier to say no when she discussed her struggles with close friends. They encouraged

---

[69]Guru Granth Sahib, Ang 1373.

[70]Bhagavad Gita, 2.14.

her and even practiced role-playing situations where she could assert her boundaries. This support made a huge difference in her confidence.

The Long-Term Benefits of Saying No

Overcoming the obstacles to 'no' yields profound benefits. It leads to greater authenticity, improved relationships, and enhanced well-being. More importantly, it empowers you to live a life aligned with your values and priorities.

1. *Empowered Decision-Making*: By mastering the art of 'no', you regain control over your time and energy. You can focus on what truly matters and make decisions that reflect your authentic self.
   'Deliberate on this fully, and then do what you wish to do.'[71]
2. *Healthier Relationships*: Setting boundaries fosters mutual respect and trust in relationships. People appreciate honesty and are more likely to respect your needs when you communicate them clearly.
3. *Increased Self-Confidence*: Each time you say no, you affirm your self-worth. This builds confidence and reinforces your ability to stand up for yourself.
4. *Improved Mental and Physical Health*: Reducing the burden of unnecessary commitments decreases stress and promotes overall well-being. It creates space for self-care, relaxation, and personal growth.

---

[71]Bhagavad Gita, 18.63.

'The wise who control their senses, mind, and intellect, and who practice yoga of action with detachment, are freed from all bondage.'[72]

Saying no is a skill that requires courage, practice, and self-awareness. It is not merely about refusing requests but about asserting your right to live a life that aligns with your values and priorities. By overcoming the fear and resistance associated with 'no', you unlock a world of possibilities for personal growth, healthier relationships, and a more fulfilling life. Embrace the power of 'no' and watch how it transforms your world.

▪

Learning to say no is a crucial life skill that can greatly enhance personal well-being and work performance.

However, many people find it difficult to decline requests due to fears and societal pressures. Understanding and addressing the barriers to saying no is key to living a more balanced and authentic life.

Several factors contribute to the hesitation in saying no. The fear of rejection often leads individuals to agree to requests they cannot fulfil, worrying they might lose professional respect or personal connections. This is particularly common in workplaces where cooperation is valued.

Similarly, people avoid saying no to evade potential conflicts, assuming that rejection will damage relationships. Another significant barrier is the fear of being judged. Societal norms frequently reward self-sacrifice, making individuals feel guilty for setting boundaries. Moreover, a fear of missed

[72]Katha Upanishad 2.1.1.

opportunities, or FOMO, often compels people to say yes even when the commitment may not align with their goals.

Avoiding 'no' comes at a high emotional cost. Constantly prioritizing others' needs can lead to burnout, chronic stress, and a loss of personal identity. When people feel pressured to say yes all the time, they often lose sight of their own values and passions, creating resentment toward both others and themselves. Over time, this erodes the quality of relationships, as hidden frustration becomes apparent.

To overcome these challenges, self-awareness is a critical first step. By identifying one's personal limits, values, and priorities, individuals can make more intentional choices about when to say no. Reframing no as a positive act that safeguards one's well-being rather than a rejection can be empowering. Developing assertiveness skills, learning to communicate boundaries respectfully, can make saying no less intimidating.

Small steps, such as practicing in low-stakes situations, build confidence over time. Incorporating techniques like the 'positive No' can help maintain goodwill. This approach involves politely declining a request while offering an alternative or expressing appreciation. Additionally, embracing discomfort as part of the growth process is essential. Saying no may feel awkward initially, but with time, it becomes easier.

The long-term benefits of mastering no are profound. It allows for better decision-making, focusing energy on what truly matters. Healthy boundaries foster respect and improve relationships, as people appreciate honesty and clear communication. Moreover, regularly asserting oneself builds self-confidence and reduces stress, leading to improved mental and physical health.

Ultimately, learning to say no is about reclaiming control over one's life. By overcoming internal and external barriers, individuals can create space for personal growth, deeper relationships, and a more meaningful existence. The power of no lies in its ability to open doors to a life aligned with one's true self.

14

No as a Pathway to a Purposeful Life

A no uttered from the deepest conviction is better than a yes merely uttered to please, or worse, to avoid trouble.

—Mahatma Gandhi, Young India, 1924

In today's interconnected world, the power of saying no is often undervalued. Many of us feel compelled to say yes to every opportunity, invitation, or demand, believing that doing so reflects ambition, kindness, or social responsibility. However, perpetually saying yes can lead to burnout, stress, and a diluted sense of purpose.

Paradoxically, the ability to say no can be transformative, enabling individuals to lead a more intentional, focused, and purposeful life. In this essay, we will explore how saying no fosters clarity, strengthens personal boundaries, cultivates self-awareness, and ultimately paves the way to a more meaningful existence.

Understanding the Culture of Yes

Modern society often equates being busy with success. People are encouraged to seize every opportunity, attend every meeting, and fulfil every request, fearing that refusal might lead to missed chances or social rejection. This culture of yes is reinforced by technology, which keeps us constantly connected and accessible. Emails, social media notifications, and instant messages demand immediate attention, making it difficult to decline even trivial engagements. However, this over commitment comes at a cost.

By saying yes to everything, people often spread themselves too thin, leaving little time for reflection, rest, or personal growth. Over time, this can result in exhaustion and dissatisfaction, as individuals lose sight of their true priorities. In contrast, learning to say no can serve as a counterbalance, helping to restore focus and align actions with values.

When Ramesh joined a tech firm, he believed that saying yes to every task would earn him respect. Over time, his workload piled up, leaving him exhausted and unable to deliver quality work. Eventually, his manager advised him to prioritize tasks. Learning to say no when needed helped Ramesh regain control of his schedule and improve his performance. This taught him that selective decision-making is key to sustaining both productivity and well-being.

Psychologists have studied the impact of over commitment and found that individuals who frequently say yes to tasks they find unimportant experience higher levels of anxiety and lower levels of satisfaction. This underscores the importance of selective decision-making in both personal and professional contexts. A study published in the *Journal of Personality and Social Psychology* highlights that those who learn to say no without guilt tend to exhibit greater emotional resilience and overall well-being.[73]

Interestingly, cultural differences influence how people perceive and practice saying no. In individualistic societies, personal boundaries are often prioritized, whereas in collectivist cultures, social harmony may take precedence over personal desires. This contrast emphasizes the need for cultural sensitivity when setting boundaries and learning to say no.

The Role of Clarity in a Purposeful Life

One of the key benefits of saying no is that it brings clarity. Purposeful living requires an understanding of one's goals, values, and priorities. However, when people overcommit, their vision becomes clouded by external demands, leaving them unsure of where to direct their energy.

Saying no forces individuals to assess their commitments and decide what truly matters.

For example, a professional aiming to advance their career may need to decline social invitations that detract from their time for skill development or networking. Similarly, a parent prioritizing quality time with family might refuse additional work projects that encroach on evenings and weekends. By saying no, they create space for the activities that align with their deeper aspirations.

The *Brihadaranyaka Upanishad* offers a profound insight with the phrase, '*Neti, neti*'[74] (Not this, not this), emphasizing

---

[73]Esterling, Ashley W., et al. 'The Psychological Costs of Saying Yes: When Agreeableness Is Associated with Lower Well-Being.' *Journal of Personality and Social Psychology*, Vol. 115, No. 3, 2018, pp. 500–520.

[74]Brihadaranyaka Upanishad, Verse 4.4.22.

the importance of discernment in life. Just as spiritual seekers reject distractions to find ultimate truth, individuals must learn to say no to what does not serve their higher purpose.

Moreover, clarity in purpose fosters better time management. Time, being a finite resource, must be allocated wisely.

Sneha, a young architect, frequently took on projects beyond her capacity, hoping to grow her portfolio. However, she felt overwhelmed and lost sight of her personal goals. She decided to refuse projects that didn't align with her vision. This allowed her to focus on a few meaningful projects, resulting in higher satisfaction and better outcomes. Saying no helped Sneha find clarity, manage her time wisely, and work towards her long-term goals.

When individuals understand what is essential, they can dedicate their limited hours to tasks that provide long-term value rather than short-term gratification. We must understand the importance of saying no to low-priority tasks to focus on high-impact goals.

Strengthening Personal Boundaries

Setting boundaries is essential for maintaining mental and emotional well-being. When people struggle to say no, they often sacrifice their own needs to accommodate others, leading to resentment and a diminished sense of autonomy. Conversely, asserting oneself through a firm no demonstrates self-respect and fosters healthier relationships.

Boundaries protect individuals from overextension and allow them to operate within their limits. For instance, declining extra responsibilities at work can prevent burnout, while refusing to engage in toxic relationships preserves emotional health. Establishing these boundaries through the power of no sends a clear message. Your time, energy, and well-being are valuable and deserve to be protected.

In a modern context, learning to establish boundaries also means recognizing when tasks or relationships drain more energy than they contribute.

It requires continuous evaluation and the courage to distance oneself from such engagements. Clinical psychologist Dr Henry Cloud, in his book *Boundaries: When to Say Yes, How to Say No to Take Control of Your Life,*[75] explains that boundaries are a form of self-care and essential for maintaining healthy relationships.

Neha, a schoolteacher, found herself constantly helping colleagues after hours. As her own workload increased, she began feeling frustrated. One day, she politely declined additional tasks, explaining her limits. Surprisingly, her colleagues understood, and she felt a sense of relief. Setting boundaries not only improved her well-being but also enhanced her teaching quality. Neha learned that saying no is an act of self-respect and a way to protect personal energy.

Moreover, setting boundaries involves not just verbal refusals but also non-verbal cues and actions. For example, maintaining a strict work schedule, turning off notifications during personal time, and delegating tasks when necessary are effective ways to reinforce personal limits.

---

[75]Cloud, Henry, and John Townsend. *Boundaries: When to Say Yes, How to Say No to Take Control of Your Life*. Zondervan, 1992.

Cultivating Self-Awareness through Reflection

Saying no encourages introspection and self-awareness, which are crucial components of purposeful living. Every no is a decision that requires evaluating one's priorities and values. This process of reflection helps individuals identify what is truly meaningful to them.

For example, consider an entrepreneur who receives multiple offers for business partnerships. By saying no to ventures that conflict with their vision or ethics, they clarify their brand identity and strengthen their commitment to their long-term goals. Similarly, a person declining a social event to spend time alone may gain insights into their need for solitude and self-care. Each decision to say no provides an opportunity to better understand oneself and align actions with inner purpose.

The Bhagavad Gita reinforces this notion: 'Better is one's own duty, though devoid of merit, than the duty of another well discharged.'[76] By staying true to one's path and rejecting distractions, individuals find clarity and fulfilment.

Raj, a startup founder, was bombarded with partnership offers. Initially, he accepted most of them, thinking they were necessary for growth. After several failed collaborations, he started reflecting on his goals. By declining partnerships that didn't align with his values, Raj gained clarity on his brand's identity and purpose. Every no made him more self-aware, helping him stay true to his vision. Over time, his business thrived on focused growth.

---

[76]Bhagavad Gita, 3.35.

Furthermore, self-awareness cultivated through thoughtful refusals enables people to recognize patterns in their behaviour. Over time, they become better equipped to prioritize and make decisions that align with their long-term aspirations. Journaling is a powerful tool for cultivating this self-awareness, allowing individuals to reflect on the reasons behind their choices and gain deeper insights into their emotional responses.

Embracing the Fear of Disapproval

One of the greatest obstacles to saying no is the fear of disapproval.

People often worry that declining requests will disappoint others or damage relationships. This fear can be especially pronounced in professional settings, where saying no might be perceived as a lack of dedication, or in personal relationships, where it might seem unkind.

However, the fear of disapproval is often exaggerated.

In many cases, people respect and appreciate those who set clear boundaries. Saying no with kindness and clarity can even strengthen relationships by fostering open communication and mutual respect. Moreover, the temporary discomfort of saying no is far outweighed by the long-term benefits of living authentically and intentionally.

Brene Brown, in her work *The Gifts of Imperfection*, highlights the courage it takes to set boundaries: 'Daring to set boundaries is about having the courage to love ourselves, even when we risk disappointing others.'[77]

---

[77]Brown, Brené. *The Gifts of Imperfection: Let Go of Who You Think. You're Supposed to Be and Embrace Who You Are*. Hazelden, 2010.

Recognizing that the world cannot be pleased always is liberating. It shifts the focus from external validation to internal fulfilment, where decisions are guided by personal values rather than societal pressures.

Saying no can also foster deeper respect in relationships. When individuals are honest about their limitations, they encourage others to do the same, creating an environment of mutual respect and understanding.

Saying No as a Tool for Growth

Saying no not only helps individuals protect their time and energy but also fosters personal and professional growth.

By refusing tasks that do not align with their strengths or interests, people can focus on developing their skills and pursuing meaningful opportunities. For instance, a writer might decline requests to edit technical documents in order to concentrate on crafting creative content, thereby honing their unique talent. Similarly, a student might turn down extracurricular activities that conflict with their academic goals, allowing them to excel in their studies. By saying no to distractions, individuals create room for growth and mastery in areas that truly matter to them.

In professional environments, growth often stems from deep work, the ability to focus without distraction on cognitively demanding tasks. Saying no to low-value activities allows professionals to enter a state of flow, thereby enhancing productivity and job satisfaction.

Additionally, saying no can lead to innovative thinking.

Vikas, an aspiring writer, was asked to manage his office's blog. Though tempted, he declined, knowing it would divert him from his novel. His friends criticized him, but he stayed firm. Months later, Vikas published his book, which received critical acclaim. His decision to say no enabled him to focus on what mattered most. This experience showed him that purposeful refusals pave the way for personal and professional growth.

When individuals prioritize essential tasks and decline unnecessary ones, they free up mental space to explore creative solutions. This approach has been adopted by leaders in various industries, who emphasize the importance of deep focus and the courage to eliminate distractions.

The Empowerment of Choice

At its core, saying no is an act of empowerment. It reminds individuals that they have control over their lives and the ability to make choices that serve their best interests. This sense of control is essential for a purposeful life, as it enables people to take ownership of their paths and confidently navigate challenges.

When individuals embrace the power of no, they no longer feel like passive participants in their lives. Instead, they become active decision-makers, capable of steering their journey in the direction of their dreams. This empowerment fosters a sense of fulfilment and reinforces the belief that they are capable of shaping their destiny.

Meera, a mother of two, juggled a full-time job and household responsibilities. Constantly asked to volunteer at her children's school, she felt drained. One day, she decided to say no to additional commitments. Though difficult, the decision empowered her to take charge of her life. She used the saved time to relax and bond with her kids. Meera realized that saying no isn't about rejection but about making choices that matter.

By rejecting societal pressures, individuals reclaim their personal freedom and authenticity. Moreover, the empowerment derived from saying no extends beyond the individual. It sets an example for others, inspiring them to prioritize their well-being and live with greater intentionality.

In summary, saying no is a tool for clarity, boundary-setting, self-awareness, and personal growth. It is not about rejection but about making mindful choices that lead to a purposeful and empowered life.

I would encourage everyone to reflect on how learning to say no can improve both their personal lives and professional journeys.

15

Sixty Strategies to Say No

A man who cannot say no to his desires,
is like a chariot with untrained horses,
difficult to control.

—Valmiki Ramayana, Ayodhya Kanda, 2.40

Saying no is a vital skill for maintaining boundaries, prioritizing personal needs, and fostering respect in relationships. While it may seem challenging, mastering the art of refusal can lead to greater clarity and confidence.

'An uncontrolled mind acts as your enemy, while a controlled mind becomes your friend.'[78] I have outlined 60 practical strategies to say no, each explained with examples to help you integrate them into your daily life.

Direct and Clear Communication

1. Be Direct: Say 'no' clearly and confidently without ambiguity. By way of example, you could state, 'I understand the opportunity, but I must decline to stay aligned with my current priorities.'

[78]Mahabharata, Shanti Parva, Chapter 177, Verse 25.

2. State Your Reason: Provide a concise and truthful reason for your refusal. 'I cannot take on this project because my schedule is fully committed for the next two weeks,' will give the message clearly.
3. Use 'I' Statements: Always express your decision from your perspective. 'I am sorry, I don't feel comfortable participating in this discussion or this project' or 'I am sorry I do not agree with the direction we are heading in.'
4. Avoid Over-Explaining: A short and straightforward 'no' can often be sufficient to convey your message. 'Thank you for thinking of me, but I must decline. I wish you all the best,' is generally enough

Polite Refusal

5. Appreciate the Offer: Show gratitude while declining. A nice way to decline could be 'Thank you for considering me, but I am unable to commit at this time.'
6. Say No with Empathy: Acknowledge the other person's situation. 'I see how important this is to you, but I need to prioritize other commitments.'
7. Compliment Before Refusing: Offering a compliment before your refusal should go down well. 'This sounds like an amazing opportunity, but I'll have to pass this time around.'
8. Suggest Alternatives: Recommend someone else or an alternative solution. 'I can't help you, but I think Ram might be a great fit for this.' You should state this and state that this is just your view and

that Ram would need to take a call based upon his circumstances.

Time Management

9. Prioritize Your Schedule: Explain your pre-existing commitments without over explaining or sounding apologetic. 'I have other deadlines I'm working on, so I can't add more to my plate right now.'
10. Use Scheduling Conflicts: Let them know your calendar does not allow it. A simple response 'I'd love to help, but my schedule is packed this week,' should be sufficient communication.
11. Ask for Time to Decide: If you think you may be able to help, request a moment to evaluate your priorities. 'Let me think it over and get back to you. If I can't help, I will let you know.'
12. Decline Future Commitments: It is always a good practice to set boundaries for upcoming opportunities. By stating 'I am not taking on any new commitments for the rest of the year' you are ensuring that your message is clear,

Emotional Boundaries

13. Value Self-Care: Emphasize your personal well-being. 'I need to focus on my health, so I will have to say no this time.'
14. Avoid Guilt: Guilt is possibly the most common reason why we say yes when we actually want to say no. Recognize your right to decline without

remorse. 'I can't commit to this, but thank you for understanding my need to prioritize.'

15. Be Firm Yet Kind: Assert your boundaries with kindness. Stating 'I appreciate the invite, but I'll have to politely decline,' conveys your message and should not upset the other person.
16. Detach Emotionally: Don't let personal feelings cloud your decision to say no. What will the other person feel is a sure sign that you are beginning to weaken and may end up taking on something you do not wish to. 'This decision isn't personal; it's about ensuring I have the bandwidth to focus on my goals.'

Work-Related Declines

17. Decline Additional Work: It is always easier to explain workload limitations to colleagues. They are also in a similar situation and should understand. 'I have existing projects that require my attention, so I can't take on additional work.'
18. Redirect Tasks: At work, there is always the possibility to guide the requester to appropriate resources. 'This task might be better suited for someone in the operations team.' It is safer not to name someone specifically.
19. Cite Organizational Policies: When requested to take on additional work, see if you can use rules or policies to back your decision. 'Our policy doesn't allow us to take additional requests of this nature.'
20. Offer Partial Assistance: Help in a limited capacity if feasible may be acceptable. However, this help should

only be offered if you have the time and the resources. 'I can't commit to the entire task, but I'm happy to contribute to the brainstorming session.'

Family & Friends

21. Set Expectations: When it comes to family and friends, it is better to clarify your priorities to avoid misunderstanding. Stating 'I can't make it to dinner because I need to prepare for a work presentation,' should be understood by most people.
22. Say No to Lending: When it comes to money matters it is always better to avoid uncomfortable financial situations. By way of example, 'I'm sorry, I can't lend you money, but I'm here to support you in other ways' should suffice.
23. Politely Decline Invitations: Be transparent and honest about your availability. 'I'm so sorry, but I can't make it to the event this weekend.' Giving this as a reason and then be seen at another event may not go down well!
24. Avoid Overcommitting: Maintain a balance in personal relationships. 'I wish I could help, but I already have plans with my family.'

Leveraging Humour

25. Use Light-hearted Humour: 'My calendar says no, and it's being very strict about it,' is a nice way to decline with a touch of humour.
26. Playfully Deflect: Lighten the mood with a joke. 'I'd

say yes, but I think my clone is on vacation.' Use this only if you can get away with a playful deflection. If you have a very serious demeanour at work, it may be best to avoid this strategy.

27. Inject Positivity: Make the refusal uplifting. 'I'd love to, but if I clone myself, I promise you'll be the first to know,' could be an excellent way to communicate the message.
28. Laugh It Off: Diffuse the awkwardness of saying no with humour. By way of example, 'I would help, but my to-do list might stage a protest.'

Cultural Considerations

29. Use Local Politeness Norms: Frame refusals that are culturally appropriate. 'In Japanese culture, saying "chotto muzukashii" softens the refusal, and I must use it here "chotto muzukashii"—it is going to be difficult.'
30. Emphasize Mutual Respect: Make you refusal sound like a shared understanding. 'Your time is valuable, and so is mine. I must respectfully say decline.'
31. Invoke Family Traditions: You could also use family obligations as a reason. By way of example, 'I can't join because we always reserve Sundays for family dinners,' is a reason no one can argue about.
32. Use Proverbs: Sometimes anchoring our refusal with a quote works well. 'As they say, "You can't pour from an empty cup," so I need to focus on replenishing my energy.'

Digital Declines

33. Leverage Email Templates: Prepare a template of a set of declines when you are communicating digitally using whichever platform. A standard response I use is 'Thank you for reaching out, but I'm not able to accommodate this request at this time.'
34. Use Auto-Responders: We can set boundaries in our inbox. 'My autoreply, which keeps changing depending on my work commitment could be, "I'm unavailable for new projects until next month" or "Please contact me after 3 months if you are still interested in involving me."'
35. Limit Social Media Requests: Decline requests for engagement politely online. 'I appreciate your message, but I'm not available to collaborate on this,' or 'Thank you for your message. I am, unfortunately tied up and regret my inability to participate. I wish the event all success.'
36. Reply Later: It is always a good idea to delay your response to avoid impulse agreements or acceptances you may regret later. A simple response 'Thank you for your message. I will need to review my commitments before responding.'

Redirecting Energy

37. Offer Future Availability: Subject to your time availability, you could commit to helping later. A straightforward response 'I can't assist right now,

but I'll be happy to in 3 months,' could be an acceptable response.

38. Suggest a Time Trade-Off: If a senior person asks you for help, you could respond by communicating the need to balance competing priorities. 'I would need to drop another task to take this on. Are you okay with that?'
39. Offer General Guidance: Provide help without full involvement. This would be a sub optimal response but if you have the time and the requester is willing, you could state, 'I can't join the team, but I'm happy to share resources to help you get started.'
40. Create Distance: Distancing yourself physically or mentally is another strategy that you could consider using. 'I'm travelling, so I won't be able to participate in this project,' is a simple and straight forward response.

Handling Persistence

41. Repeat Your Refusal: If the requester persists, stick to your initial no without elaboration or explanation. 'As I mentioned earlier, I won't be able to help this time. Thanks for your understanding.'
42. Use a Broken Record Technique: Calmly repeat your response if pressured repeatedly. 'I am sorry but I still have to decline. My commitments have not changed.'
43. Acknowledge the Frustration: Empathize without altering your decision. 'I see this is important to you, but I sincerely hope you will understand

that I am not able to take this on because of my commitments.'

44. Set Boundaries Firmly: Make it clear that persistence won't change your decision. A firm statement—'I've already shared my decision, and I need you to respect it'—should get the message across.

Empowering Others

45. Encourage Independence: Suggest they manage without your help. 'I trust you've got this handled. You don't need my input.' This should be used only if you believe you have the 'stature' at work to make this statement. You cannot make this statement to someone senior to you!
46. Delegate Responsibility: Delegation is always a great alternative if you have the authority to delegate. Point them to someone else who can assist. 'I can't help, but Meena is great at these tasks and might be able to step in.'
47. Provide Resources: Guide the person making the request to tools or resources instead of direct help. 'I can't assist directly, but here's a great article that addresses this issue and may be of some help to you.'
48. Foster Skill Development: Encourage them to solve the problem themselves. 'This is a great opportunity for you to learn this process. Let me know how it goes.' As stated earlier, this should be used only if you believe you have the 'stature' at work to make this statement. You cannot make this statement to someone senior to you!

Healthy Work-Life Balance

49. Protect Personal Time: Assert the need for downtime for yourself. Most people understand the need for work-life balance and should normally not be unreasonable while making the request. 'I've planned some personal time this evening, so I won't be able to join.'
50. Limit Out-of-Hours Work: We need to develop the capability to decline tasks outside our work hours. 'I'm happy to discuss this during work hours, but I can't address it now.' This statement could be culturally acceptable in some parts of the world and not in others.
51. Turn Off Notifications: Avoid responding to requests immediately. 'My policy is to disconnect after 7 pm, so I'll review this tomorrow.' For several years now, I do not look at my phone after 7 pm. In a short period of time, most people understood that if they could not communicate with me before 7 pm, they should expect a response from me very early the next morning.
52. Emphasize Rest: Highlight the importance of recovery. Do not hesitate to state 'I need to recharge to perform my best, so I'll have to skip this.'

Philosophical Approaches

53. Invoke Bigger Goals: Cite alignment with your values or goals to communicate your inability to take on any additional work. 'This does not align with my goals right now, so I will have to decline.'

54. Use Long-Term Perspective: Focus on future benefits of saying no. Colleagues should understand if you state 'Saying no now helps me ensure I'm available for larger opportunities ahead.'
55. Reflect on Priorities: Reframe the situation in light of your priorities. 'I have committed to focusing on my family this month, so I cannot add more to my plate for the moment.'
56. Learn from Past Overcommitments: Share a lesson from previous experiences with the person requesting for your help or assistance. 'I've taken on too much in the past, and I'm learning to set better boundaries.'

Using Silence Strategically

57. Pause Before Answering: Take a moment to think before responding. Sometimes a knee jerk response gets us into a situation we may not have bargained for. 'Let me take a moment to think about this. On second thoughts, I won't be able to.'
58. Let Silence Speak: Stay silent to subtly imply a no. Silence is an easy way to communicate. After a long pause, you could say, 'I think you can find another way to resolve this.'
59. Use Non-Verbal Communication: Shake your head or use a gentle smile to decline. By way of example smile politely and say, 'I appreciate the ask, but I'm not able to help.'

60. Leave the Door Open for Silence: Avoid responding immediately, letting the lack of commitment suffice. One way to leave the door open for a future review is: 'I'll think about it and get back to you if possible.'

16

Real-Life Stories of Empowerment

Through Saying No

Nothing can explain the power of 'no' or empowering oneself or many people by using no as a tool. This has been seen many times around the world.

I have attempted to highlight a few examples from multiple sectors from around the world. These examples simply tell us how we need conviction, self-confidence and the willingness to take responsibility if our decision to say no is incorrect.

Business Leaders

1. **Ratan Tata Says No to the Sale of Tata Group's Car Business (India, 1999)**[79]
   In 1999, Tata Motors was struggling, and Ratan Tata approached Ford to sell the company's car division. During the negotiation, Ford's executives insulted

[79]Tata, Ratan. Interviews and Tata Group corporate history.

Tata, suggesting they were doing him a favour by considering the purchase. Tata walked away, saying no to the deal.

A few years later, Tata Motors turned around its fortunes and, in a twist of fate, acquired Ford's Jaguar and Land Rover brands in 2008. By refusing to accept an unfair deal, Ratan Tata preserved the dignity of his organization and later transformed it into a global automotive powerhouse.

2. **Steve Jobs Says No to Mediocrity (USA, 1980s-2010s)**[80]

   Steve Jobs, co-founder of Apple Inc., was known for his insistence on perfection and simplicity in product design. Throughout his career, he was famous for saying no to ideas and products that didn't meet his high standards. Whether it was the user interface of the Macintosh, the design of the iPod, or the features of the iPhone, Jobs believed that a few well-crafted products could change the world.

   He once said, 'Innovation is saying no to a thousand things.' By rejecting mediocrity and refusing to compromise on quality, Jobs helped Apple create iconic products that redefined industries. His story underscores that saying 'no' can be a critical part of achieving excellence. By focusing on fewer, better products, Apple grew into one of the most valuable companies in the world, with a loyal customer base inspired by its founder's vision.

[80]Isaacson, Walter. *Steve Jobs*. Simon & Schuster, 2011; Apple corporate history.

3. **Richard Branson Says No to the Status Quo (UK, 1970s)**[81]
   Richard Branson, founder of the Virgin Group, built his career by challenging conventional thinking. When he launched Virgin Atlantic in 1984, the airline industry was dominated by a few large players who maintained rigid customer service standards. Branson said no to the status quo by introducing innovations such as in-flight entertainment, better food, and a customer-centric approach.
   His boldness wasn't limited to aviation; Branson also disrupted industries like music, telecommunications, and even space travel with Virgin Galactic. Despite facing scepticism and numerous setbacks, Branson's refusal to conform allowed him to build a brand known for its creativity and customer focus. His story demonstrates that saying no to traditional methods can create opportunities for ground-breaking innovation and success.
4. **Arianna Huffington's Decision to Say No to Overwork (USA, 2007)**[82]
   In 2007, Arianna Huffington, founder of *The Huffington Post*, was a successful media executive juggling multiple responsibilities. One day, she collapsed from exhaustion, hitting her head on her

---

[81]Branson, Richard. *Losing My Virginity*. Crown Publishing, 1998; Virgin Group corporate history. Ratan Tata's interviews and Tata Group's corporate history.

[82]Huffington, Arianna. *Thrive*. Harmony Books, 2014; Thrive Global initiatives.

desk and breaking her cheekbone. This incident served as a wake-up call, leading her to rethink the value of relentless work culture. Huffington decided to say no to overwork and burnout, prioritizing health and well-being instead.

She transformed her lifestyle and launched Thrive Global, a company dedicated to promoting well-being in work places. Through her advocacy, Huffington has helped shift the narrative around work-life balance, encouraging individuals and organizations to embrace healthier practices. Her story highlights that saying no to harmful societal norms can lead to personal transformation and inspire systemic change.

5. **Dr Devi Shetty Says No to Expensive Healthcare (India, 2001)[83]**

   Dr Devi Shetty, a renowned cardiac surgeon, noticed that life-saving surgeries were unaffordable for many Indians. Determined to make healthcare accessible, he founded Narayana Health in 2001, focusing on low-cost, high-volume surgical procedures.

   By saying no to the traditional high-cost healthcare model, Dr Shetty was able to drastically reduce the cost of heart surgeries while maintaining world-class quality. His innovative approach has provided affordable healthcare to millions of underprivileged patients in India and beyond.

[83]Interviews with Dr Devi Shetty and Narayana Health case studies.

Social Sector Leaders

1. **Nand Kishore Chaudhary Says No to Exploitative Middlemen in the Carpet Industry (India, 1978)**[84]
   In the late 1970s, Nand Kishore Chaudhary founded Jaipur Rugs with a mission to provide sustainable livelihoods to rural artisans in India. At the time, the hand-knotted carpet industry was plagued by exploitative middlemen who controlled wages and working conditions for weavers.
   Chaudhary said no to this system by bypassing middlemen and directly working with artisans. He not only ensured fair wages but also empowered women and marginalized communities by offering them skill development and financial independence. Today, Jaipur Rugs is a global social enterprise with over 40,000 artisans across India. By rejecting exploitative practices, Chaudhary revolutionized the carpet industry and demonstrated how ethical entrepreneurship can drive both profit and social impact.
2. **Kalpana Saroj Says No to Poverty and Injustice (India, 1980s)**[85]
   Born into a Dalit family in rural Maharashtra, Kalpana Saroj faced extreme poverty and discrimination. Married off at a young age, she endured abuse but eventually left her husband, saying no to a life of oppression. With minimal education and resources,

[84]Interviews with Nand Kishore Chaudhary and Jaipur Rugs case studies.
[85]Speeches and media interviews of Kalpana Saroj.

she worked tirelessly and gradually built a business empire.

Today, she is the Chairperson of Kamani Tubes, turning around a dying company into a thriving enterprise. Saroj's story is a powerful example of how saying no to societal limitations can lead to remarkable success.

3. **Malala Yousafzai's Fight for Girls' Education (Pakistan, 2012)**[86]

   In the Swat Valley of Pakistan, under Taliban control, girls were forbidden from attending school. Malala Yousafzai, a young girl with a passion for learning, refused to accept this. At just 11 years old, she began writing a blog for the BBC Urdu service under a pseudonym, describing life under Taliban rule and the challenges faced by girls who wanted an education. Despite the danger, Malala continued to speak out, advocating for girls' right to learn.

   On October 9, 2012, a Taliban gunman boarded her school bus and shot her in the head in an attempt to silence her. Malala survived the attack after extensive medical treatment in the UK. Instead of retreating into fear, she boldly said no to oppression by continuing her fight on a global stage. She co-founded the Malala Fund to promote education worldwide and, at 17, became the youngest Nobel Peace Prize laureate. Malala's unwavering commitment to education has empowered millions of girls to say no to discrimination.

---

[86]Yousafzai, Malala. *I Am Malala: The Girl Who Stood Up for Education and Was Shot by the Taliban.* Little, Brown and Company, 2013.

4. **Wangari Maathai Says No to Deforestation (Kenya, 1970s-2000s)**[87]

   Wangari Maathai, an environmental activist from Kenya, led the Green Belt Movement, which focused on reforestation and sustainable development. Despite facing political opposition and imprisonment, she said no to deforestation and environmental degradation.

   Her efforts resulted in the planting of over 50 million trees and earned her the Nobel Peace Prize in 2004. By rejecting short-term exploitation of natural resources, Maathai created a lasting environmental legacy.

5. **Liu Xiaobo Says No to Authoritarianism (China, 2000s)**[88]

   Liu Xiaobo, a Chinese literary critic and human rights activist, said no to authoritarian rule by openly advocating for democratic reforms in China. He was a key figure in drafting 'Charter 08', a manifesto calling for political freedom and human rights.

   Despite being imprisoned multiple times, Liu remained steadfast in his commitment to nonviolent resistance. In 2010, he was awarded the Nobel Peace Prize while still in prison. Liu's courageous no to repression inspired global human rights movements, even though it cost him his freedom.

---

[87] Maathai, Wangari. *Unbowed: A Memoir*. Alfred A. Knopf, 2006.

[88] Reports on Liu Xiaobo's activism and Nobel Peace Prize acceptance.

6. **Bhatt Says No to Exploitation of Women Workers (India, 1970s)**[89]

   In 1972, Ela Bhatt founded the Self-Employed Women's Association (SEWA) in India, an organization dedicated to empowering female workers in the informal sector. At a time when women workers had little to no rights, Bhatt said no to their exploitation by creating a platform that provided them with financial services, healthcare, and legal aid.

   Today, SEWA has over two million members and continues to fight for women's economic independence. Bhatt's story is a testament to how one person's refusal to accept inequality can uplift entire communities.

7. **Greta Thunberg Says No to Complacency (Global, 2018)**[90]

   At the age of 15, Greta Thunberg decided to take action against global climate inaction by staging a solo protest outside the Swedish Parliament. Holding a sign that read 'School Strike for Climate', she refused to attend school on Fridays until her government took more serious measures to combat climate change. What started as a lone act of defiance quickly grew into a global movement, with millions of students participating in 'Fridays for Future' strikes across the world.

   Greta's unwavering no to complacency from

[89]Interviews and SEWA's official reports.

[90]Documentaries, news articles, and interviews with Greta Thunberg.

political leaders earned her international recognition, including a nomination for the Nobel Peace Prize. Despite facing criticism and personal attacks, Greta continued to speak out at major global forums, including the United Nations Climate Action Summit, where her famous words, 'How dare you?' resonated worldwide. Her story shows that even young voices can challenge powerful institutions by simply refusing to accept the status quo.

8. **Arunachalam Muruganantham Says No to Taboos Around Menstrual Hygiene (India, 2000s)**[91]

   In rural India, menstruation was surrounded by stigma, with women often using unsafe alternatives to sanitary pads. Arunachalam Muruganantham, a school dropout from Tamil Nadu, noticed his wife struggling during her menstrual cycle and decided to find a low-cost solution. Despite facing ridicule from his community, including his own family, Muruganantham said no to societal taboos and began developing an affordable sanitary pad-making machine.

   His innovation has since empowered thousands of women to start small businesses and improved menstrual hygiene for millions across rural India. By challenging societal norms, Muruganantham not only improved public health but also sparked a conversation about menstrual dignity.

---

[91] *Period. End of Sentence.* Documentary; interviews with Arunachalam Muruganantham.

World Leaders

1. **Gandhi Says No to British Salt Laws (India, 1930)**[92]
   In 1930, under British colonial rule, the Indian people were prohibited from making or selling salt—a staple in every household. Instead, they were forced to buy heavily taxed salt from the British government. Viewing this as a symbol of colonial oppression, Mahatma Gandhi decided to say no to this unjust law by organizing the Salt March, a 240-mile journey from his ashram to the coastal village of Dandi.
   Over the course of 24 days, Gandhi and thousands of his followers marched across the Indian countryside, gaining support and attention. Upon reaching Dandi, Gandhi collected salt from the sea, breaking the law in a symbolic act of defiance. This peaceful protest galvanized millions of Indians to join the independence movement and inspired civil disobedience campaigns worldwide. Gandhi's decision to say no to British rule using nonviolent resistance remains a powerful example of how rejecting injustice can lead to lasting change.
2. **Winston Churchill's Refusal to Negotiate with Hitler (UK, 1940s)**
   In 1940, during one of the darkest periods of World War II, Britain stood alone against the might of Nazi Germany. Many British politicians, including Lord

---

[92]Gandhi, Mohandas K. *Gandhi: An Autobiography—The Story of My Experiments with Truth.* Navajivan Publishing House, 1927; historical accounts of the Salt March.

Halifax, advocated for peace negotiations with Hitler to avoid further destruction. Winston Churchill, who had just become Prime Minister, firmly said no to any form of compromise with the Nazi regime. He believed that negotiating with a tyrant like Hitler would only result in a temporary reprieve, not lasting peace.

Churchill's refusal was not without consequence; it isolated Britain diplomatically and increased the immediate risk of invasion. However, his unyielding stance inspired his countrymen to endure the hardships of war. Churchill's defiance culminated in his iconic speech: 'We shall fight on the beaches... we shall never surrender.' His decision to say no to appeasement became a turning point in the war and solidified his legacy as a symbol of resistance against tyranny.

3. **Nelson Mandela's Refusal to Compromise on Equality (South Africa, 1990s)**

   Nelson Mandela spent 27 years in prison for his opposition to South Africa's apartheid regime. Throughout his imprisonment, he was offered conditional release multiple times, but each time he said no. The conditions required him to renounce the armed struggle and accept racial inequality, something Mandela refused to do. In 1990, he was finally released unconditionally, having stood firm on his principles.

   Even after his release, Mandela continued to say no to vengeance and hatred, insisting on peaceful negotiations and reconciliation. His stance helped

South Africa transition to a democracy without descending into civil war. Mandela's refusal to compromise on his core values led to the dismantling of apartheid and earned him a Nobel Peace Prize. His story exemplifies the power of saying no to injustice and remaining steadfast in the pursuit of equality and freedom.

4. **Abraham Lincoln's Emancipation Proclamation (USA, 1863)**

   During the American Civil War, Abraham Lincoln faced tremendous pressure from all sides. Many within his administration and the public urged him to focus solely on preserving the Union and to abandon the controversial issue of slavery. Lincoln, however, said no to the idea of a Union that permitted slavery. He believed that true unity could only be achieved by addressing the moral crisis at the heart of the conflict.

   In 1863, he issued the Emancipation Proclamation, declaring all slaves in Confederate-held territory to be free. Though it did not immediately free all slaves, it fundamentally changed the nature of the war, making it a fight for human freedom. Lincoln's bold no to compromise on the issue of slavery paved the way for the eventual abolition of slavery in the United States and solidified his place in history as a champion of liberty.

5. **Narendra Modi's Refusal to Accept Conventional Politics (India, 2001-Present)**

   Narendra Modi's political journey began with humble origins, serving as a tea seller before joining the

Rashtriya Swayamsevak Sangh (RSS) and later the Bharatiya Janata Party (BJP). When he became Chief Minister of Gujarat in 2001, many doubted his ability to lead due to his lack of political lineage. Modi said no to conventional political norms that favoured dynastic politics and instead focused on development and governance.

His refusal to follow traditional methods transformed Gujarat into an industrial powerhouse. When he became India's Prime Minister in 2014, he continued to say no to outdated political practices by emphasizing digital governance, infrastructure development, and social welfare schemes. Modi's rejection of the status quo has redefined Indian politics and governance, making him one of the most influential leaders in the country's history.

6. **Angela Merkel's Refugee Policy Decision (Germany, 2015)**

In 2015, Europe faced a major refugee crisis as millions fled war-torn regions in the Middle East and Africa. While many European leaders closed their borders, Angela Merkel said no to exclusion and fear. She adopted an open-door policy, allowing over a million refugees to enter Germany. Merkel's decision was met with both praise and criticism.

Supporters saw it as a humanitarian act, while opponents feared it would strain Germany's resources and fuel xenophobia. Despite the backlash, Merkel remained steadfast, saying, 'We can do this.' Her stance on the refugee crisis not only demonstrated compassion but also highlighted her commitment to

European unity and human rights. By refusing to bow to political pressure, Merkel set an example of moral leadership in the face of adversity.

7. **Rosa Parks Refuses to Give Up Her Seat (USA, 1955)**[93]

   On December 1, 1955, Rosa Parks, a 42-year-old African American seamstress, made a decision that would change the course of American history. She boarded a bus in Montgomery, Alabama, and took a seat in the 'coloured' section. When the white section of the bus filled up, the driver demanded that Rosa, along with three other Black passengers, give up their seats. While the other passengers complied, Rosa firmly said no and remained seated.

   This simple yet powerful act of defiance led to her arrest and a $10 fine. Rosa's quiet courage wasn't merely about refusing to stand; it was about rejecting a system that perpetuated racial inequality. Her arrest sparked outrage and led to the Montgomery Bus Boycott, a 381-day protest that crippled the city's public transportation system and became a pivotal moment in the Civil Rights Movement. Rosa's story continues to inspire countless individuals to stand up for justice by simply saying no.

8. **Tsai Ing-wen Says No to Political Intimidation (Taiwan, 2020)**[94]

   Tsai Ing-wen, the first female President of Taiwan,

[93]Parks, Rosa, and Douglas Brinkley. *Rosa Parks: My Story.* Puffin Books, 1992.

[94]Interviews and news reports on Tsai Ing-wen's presidency.

faced immense pressure from China, which views Taiwan as a breakaway province. Despite military threats and diplomatic isolation, Tsai said no to political intimidation by standing firm on Taiwan's sovereignty.

Under her leadership, Taiwan has strengthened its democracy and built global alliances. Her defiance in the face of adversity has made her a symbol of resilience and effective leadership in Asia.

Scriptures

1. **Nachiketa Says No to Temptation (Katha Upanishad)**

   Nachiketa, a young boy in the Katha Upanishad, is known for his unwavering resolve in the pursuit of truth. Sent to the abode of Yama, the god of death, Nachiketa asks for knowledge about what happens after death. Yama tries to dissuade him by offering wealth, power, and long life.

   Nachiketa, however, says no to these temptations, recognizing that material gains are temporary. His steadfast refusal impresses Yama, who ultimately imparts the profound knowledge of the Self and the nature of immortality. Nachiketa's story teaches the importance of saying no to distractions and staying focused on one's higher purpose.
2. **Sita's Refusal to Return with Hanuman (Ramayana)**

   In the epic Ramayana, when Hanuman finds Sita imprisoned in Ravana's palace, he offers to carry her back to Rama. Sita, however, says no to this offer, insisting that Rama must come to rescue her and fulfil his duty as a husband and warrior.

Her refusal is not born out of helplessness but out of a deep understanding of dharma (duty) and the importance of Rama's role in defeating evil. Sita's decision underscores the power of saying no to easy solutions and the importance of adhering to principles.

3. **Draupadi's Refusal to Submit to Humiliation (Mahabharata)**

   During the infamous dice game in the Mahabharata, Draupadi is dragged into the court and humiliated by the Kauravas. When she is ordered to disrobe, she says no to submitting to such indignity. Instead, she appeals to the elders and questions the legitimacy of the game that led to her being staked.

   Her defiance leads to divine intervention, and Krishna protects her honour. Draupadi's refusal to accept injustice becomes a catalyst for the Kurukshetra war and highlights the power of standing up against wrong, even in the face of overwhelming odds.

4. **Shivaji's Refusal to Bow to Aurangzeb (Maratha Empire)**

   Shivaji Maharaj, the founder of the Maratha Empire, is celebrated for his defiance against the Mughal emperor Aurangzeb. Captured and held in Delhi, Shivaji was pressured to bow before Aurangzeb and accept his authority. Shivaji said no to submission and instead orchestrated a daring escape. His refusal to surrender not only preserved the Maratha spirit of independence but also inspired future generations to resist tyranny. Shivaji's story exemplifies the power of saying no to oppression and asserting one's right to freedom.

Entertainment/Sports

1. **Gemma Arterton's Stand Against Coercion in Hollywood**
   British actress Gemma Arterton is known for her strong will and refusal to be bullied into uncomfortable situations on set. In an interview, Arterton revealed that during a film shoot, a powerful director tried to coerce her into performing an explicit scene that was not part of the original agreement. Despite the pressure and potential risk to her career, Arterton said no and stood her ground. She later advocated for greater use of intimacy coordinators in the industry to protect actors' comfort and consent. Arterton's bold stance empowered not only herself but also inspired younger actors to speak up when faced with inappropriate demands. Her refusal to bow to industry pressure highlights the importance of personal boundaries in professional environments, particularly in the entertainment industry.
2. **Anil Kapoor's Fight Against Unauthorized Use of His Likeness**
   In an age where digital media manipulation is rampant, Bollywood actor Anil Kapoor took a significant stand by saying no to the unauthorized use of his image through artificial intelligence. Distorted videos and images bearing Kapoor's likeness were

circulating on the internet, without his permission or control.

Kapoor filed a case in the New Delhi High Court, leading to a landmark ruling in his favour, which prohibited the misuse of his persona. His refusal to allow unchecked exploitation of his image rights not only protected his brand but also set a legal precedent for other actors. Kapoor's bold move empowered artists and public figures, urging them to safeguard their digital identities.

3. **Oprah Winfrey Says No to Tabloid TV (USA, 1990s)**[95]

   In the 1990s, daytime television in America was dominated by sensationalist talk shows that often prioritized shock value and scandal over substance. Oprah Winfrey, whose show initially mirrored this format, realized that such content didn't align with her personal values. She decided to take a risk by saying no to tabloid-style programming and shifted the focus of her show to meaningful discussions about self-improvement, spirituality, and social issues.

   Many in the media industry doubted the move, predicting a drop in ratings. However, Oprah's decision paid off, turning her show into a cultural phenomenon. By refusing to follow the trend, she built a media empire grounded in authenticity and positivity. Her story illustrates that saying no to societal pressures can lead to transformative outcomes. Oprah's bold choice empowered not

[95]Oprah Winfrey's biography and interviews.

only herself but also millions of viewers who sought inspiration and personal growth.

4. **Kangana Ranaut's Fight Against Nepotism in Bollywood**

   Kangana Ranaut is one of Bollywood's most fearless voices, known for standing up to the entrenched nepotism in the industry. By openly criticizing powerful producers and directors who favoured star kids over talented outsiders, Ranaut stirred a national debate.

   Despite facing significant backlash, she continued to say no to projects and collaborations that went against her principles. This stance not only empowered her to choose roles that aligned with her values but also inspired a generation of actors to speak out against injustice. Ranaut's journey is a testament to the power of self-respect and perseverance in the face of systemic bias.

5. **Taylor Swift's Refusal to Be Silenced by Record Labels**

   Taylor Swift, one of the world's most successful music artists, made headlines when she took a stand against her former record label, Big Machine Records. After the label refused to grant her ownership of her master recordings, Swift said no to being silenced. Instead, she re-recorded her old albums, effectively reclaiming her music.

   By refusing to accept unfair terms, Swift empowered herself and inspired countless artists to fight for their creative rights. Her decision not only boosted her career but also opened up conversations about artist ownership and intellectual property in the music industry.

6. **Zohra Sehgal Says No to Age Limits in Acting (India, 1990s–2000s)**[96]

   Zohra Sehgal, one of India's most celebrated actresses, began her Bollywood career in her late 70s, after decades of working in theatre and television. In an industry where youth is often prioritized, she said no to ageism and continued acting well into her 90s. Her vibrant performances in films like *Cheeni Kum* and *Dil Se* inspired older actors to pursue their passion without fear of societal judgment. By rejecting conventional age norms, Sehgal became a symbol of timeless talent and creativity.

7. **Serena Williams Says No to Body Shaming (Global, 2018)**[97]

   Throughout her career, Serena Williams has faced relentless scrutiny about her muscular physique, style of play, and even her choice of attire. In 2018, after she wore a black catsuit at the French Open to aid her circulation post-childbirth, officials banned the outfit, claiming it was disrespectful to the game.

   Serena responded gracefully but made it clear that she would not accept body shaming or attempts to police her clothing. She continued to break barriers by wearing outfits that represented her individuality and confidence, including tutus and bold colours, during subsequent matches. Serena's refusal to

[96]Biographical articles on Zohra Sehgal.

[97]Media coverage and Serena Williams' interviews.

conform to outdated norms empowered athletes, particularly women of colour, to embrace their uniqueness. By saying no to societal expectations, she not only revolutionized tennis but also became a global symbol of strength and self-acceptance.

8. **JK Rowling's Rejection of Quick Money Deals (UK, 2000s)**[98]

   After the immense success of the Harry Potter series, JK Rowling was inundated with offers from corporations eager to commercialize her characters through various merchandise and media ventures. While many authors might have leaped at the chance to profit, Rowling said no to deals that didn't align with her vision for the Wizarding World. She refused poorly thought-out projects that could dilute the integrity of her work, such as hastily developed spin-offs and subpar merchandise.

   This decision came at a financial cost in the short term, but it allowed her to retain creative control over her brand. Ultimately, this led to high-quality adaptations, including critically acclaimed films, immersive theme parks, and successful stage productions like *Harry Potter and the Cursed Child*. Rowling's story highlights how saying no to short-term gain can protect long-term success and creative integrity.

---

[98]JK Rowling's interviews and documentaries.

Conclusion
Embracing the Transformative Power of Saying No

He who has conquered himself is a greater hero than he who has defeated a thousand times a thousand men.

—Bhagavad Gita, Chapter 6, Verse 6

This book, *The Power of Saying NO!*, has explored a wide array of contexts—personal, professional, cultural, and philosophical, to illuminate how mastering the art of refusal can lead to profound personal growth, improved well-being, and stronger relationships.

In a world where time, energy, and personal resources are constantly stretched thin, the power of saying no becomes an invaluable tool in shaping a purposeful life.

As we conclude this exploration, it is essential to reflect on the core themes and practical wisdom that can empower readers to lead more intentional lives.

Reclaiming Control Over Your Life

At the heart of saying no is the principle of control. Too often, people find themselves overwhelmed because they have said yes to too many things—projects, obligations, and even social expectations. Saying no is an act of self-respect, a declaration that your time and energy are finite resources that should be allocated wisely.

Throughout this book, we have seen countless examples, from mythology to modern life, where individuals lost their sense of self or well-being because they felt compelled to say yes. When we say no, we assert our autonomy and reinforce the notion that our time, energy, and priorities are valuable. By doing so, we establish that our decisions are guided by intentionality rather than external pressures.

By refusing to overcommit, individuals can regain clarity about their priorities. This clarity helps in setting boundaries, which, as discussed throughout the book, is a cornerstone of a balanced and fulfilling life. Reclaiming control is not about being selfish, it is about preserving one's mental, emotional, and physical well-being.

One of the key insights from this journey is that saying no allows us to regain control over our lives. It reminds us that we are not obligated to meet every demand placed upon us. Instead, we can choose where to direct our focus and energy, ensuring that our actions align with our personal values and long-term goals.

Boundaries Are the Foundation of Healthy Relationships

Healthy relationships, whether personal or professional, are built on mutual respect, trust, and understanding. One of the greatest myths about saying no is that it damages relationships. In reality, setting boundaries through 'no' can strengthen relationships by fostering respect and open communication.

When we set clear boundaries, we teach others how we wish to be treated. This is not an act of exclusion but an invitation to engage in a relationship that respects each person's individuality. As discussed in the chapters on personal relationships, learning to say no with kindness and clarity helps us avoid resentment and emotional burnout, leading to healthier, more balanced interactions.

Contrary to popular belief, saying no can strengthen relationships rather than harm them. Clear boundaries foster respect and understanding. When people are honest about their limits, they cultivate trust and authenticity in their interactions.

In personal relationships, learning to say no can prevent resentment and emotional exhaustion. For instance, when friends or family members request too much of our time, a polite but firm refusal can help maintain harmony. Similarly, in professional settings, declining tasks that do not align with one's responsibilities or goals can enhance productivity and prevent burnout.

In professional settings, saying no can help establish credibility and focus. Leaders and employees who are clear about their limits are often more respected because they are seen as decisive and reliable. By refusing to overcommit, they ensure that they can deliver high-quality work and maintain their integrity.

Overcoming the Fear of Rejection

One of the most pervasive challenges people face when learning to say no is the fear of rejection. This fear often stems from a deep-seated need for approval and belonging.

Throughout the book, we have explored how cultural and societal expectations reinforce this fear, making it difficult for individuals to assert their boundaries.

One of the greatest obstacles to saying no is the internal struggle. The fear of rejection, guilt, and the desire for approval. These emotions are deeply ingrained, often stemming from cultural and societal conditioning. We have explored in this book, understanding the psychology behind these fears is the first step toward overcoming them. By understanding the psychology behind this fear, we can begin to overcome it.

Saying no does not equate to rejecting a person; it simply means declining a particular request. When communicated respectfully, no can be a powerful tool for maintaining self-respect while preserving relationships.

Overcoming guilt involves reframing no as an act of self-care rather than selfishness. It is about recognizing that constantly saying yes can lead to diminished well-being, which ultimately benefits no one. Similarly, addressing the fear of rejection requires acknowledging that true relationships are built on mutual respect, not constant acquiescence.

Moreover, the fear of rejection can be mitigated by reframing how we view 'no'. Instead of seeing it as a negative response, we can view it as a positive affirmation of our priorities and values. By doing so, we shift the focus from external validation to internal alignment.

Cultural Perspectives on Saying No

Culture plays a significant role in shaping how we perceive and respond to the concept of saying no. As highlighted in this book, different cultures have varying norms and expectations regarding refusal. In collectivist cultures, for instance, saying no can be perceived as disrespectful or selfish, making it even more challenging for individuals to set boundaries.

The cultural lens on saying no is significant.

In many collectivist societies, including India, saying no is often perceived as rude or disrespectful. However, as highlighted through references to ancient texts like the Bhagavad Gita the Ramayana and the Mahabharata, discernment and the ability to refuse are seen as virtues.

Yet, even within these cultural contexts, there are examples of wisdom and discernment advocating for the thoughtful use of 'no'. Ancient scriptures and philosophical teachings, such as those from the Bhagavad Gita and the Mahabharata, emphasize the importance of discernment and the courage to stand by one's principles.

By understanding these cultural nuances, we can approach the act of saying no with greater empathy and awareness. This cultural sensitivity enables us to navigate complex social dynamics while staying true to our values.

These stories teach us that saying no is not about defiance but about adhering to one's values and principles. For example, Yudhishthira's inability to say no in the Mahabharata led to dire consequences, illustrating the importance of setting limits even in difficult circumstances.

By drawing on these cultural narratives, readers can find inspiration to navigate their own challenges in saying no, especially in environments where refusal is frowned upon.

The Practical Benefits of Saying No

Beyond the philosophical and emotional dimensions, saying no offers numerous practical benefits. These include:

1. **Enhanced Productivity**: Saying no to nonessential tasks frees up time and mental space for activities that truly matter. This focused approach enhances productivity and allows us to achieve our goals more effectively.
2. **Improved Mental Health**: Constantly saying yes can lead to stress, anxiety, and burnout. By setting boundaries and prioritizing self-care, we protect our mental well-being and cultivate a healthier, more balanced lifestyle.
3. **Strengthened Decision-Making**: The ability to say no is a hallmark of strong decision making. It requires clarity about one's goals and priorities, enabling individuals to make choices that align with their long-term vision.
4. **Greater Self-Confidence**: Each time we successfully say No, we reinforce our sense of self-worth and confidence. This positive reinforcement helps us become more assertive and self-assured in our interactions.
5. **Personal and Professional Growth**: When individuals focus on what aligns with their values and goals, they experience greater satisfaction and fulfilment. This intentional approach fosters both personal and professional growth.

Strategies for Mastering the Art of Saying No

Mastering the art of saying no requires practice, patience, and persistence. Some select strategies discussed in this book include:

1. **Clear and Direct Communication**: Be clear and direct when saying no. Avoid vague responses that can lead to confusion or further requests. A simple, respectful no can often be more effective than a lengthy explanation.
2. **Using 'I' Statements**: When refusing a request, use 'I' statements to express your feelings and needs. This approach minimizes the likelihood of the other person feeling blamed or criticized.
3. **Offering Alternatives**: If appropriate, offer an alternative solution or compromise. This shows that you value the relationship and are willing to help in a way that aligns with your boundaries.
4. **Practicing Assertiveness**: Assertiveness is a skill that can be developed through practice. Start by saying no in low-stakes situations and gradually work your way up to more significant requests.
5. **Managing Guilt**: Guilt is a common emotion associated with saying no. However, it is important to remember that prioritizing your well-being is not selfish. Reframe guilt as a reminder that you are taking care of yourself.
6. **Building Resilience**: Learning to say no involves facing discomfort. Building resilience helps individuals stay firm in their decisions despite external pressures.

Embracing a Purposeful Life

Ultimately, the power of saying no lies in its ability to help individuals lead purposeful lives. By refusing what does not serve their goals, values, or well-being, they create space for what truly matters.

Living purposefully means making deliberate choices rather than being swept along by external demands. It means prioritizing quality over quantity in relationships, work, and personal pursuits. Saying no is a tool for crafting a life that reflects who you truly are.

At its core, the power of saying no is about embracing a purposeful life. It is about making conscious choices that reflect our true selves and our deepest values. By learning to say no, we create space for what truly matters, whether it is spending time with loved ones, pursuing personal passions, or simply enjoying moments of rest and reflection.

Final Thoughts

As you close this book, remember that saying no is not about negativity or rejection. It is about affirmation. Affirming your right to choose, your right to prioritize, and your right to live authentically.

This journey has been about more than just a word. It has been about reclaiming your power, setting boundaries, and embracing a life of intentionality. Whether you are navigating personal relationships, professional obligations, or societal expectations, the ability to say no will serve as a compass, guiding you toward a more balanced, fulfilling, and meaningful existence.

Let us remember the words of Steve Jobs: 'Focusing is about saying no. You have to say no to 1,000 things to make sure you don't get on the wrong track or try to do too much.'

By embracing the power of saying no, we empower ourselves to lead lives of greater focus, integrity, and meaning.

In the words of the great philosopher Epictetus:

'He who controls his desires, controls his destiny.'

May you find the courage to say no when it matters most, and may that courage lead you to a life of clarity, purpose, and inner peace.

As you move forward, may you find the strength to say no when it matters most, the wisdom to discern when to say yes, and the courage to live a life that is true to yourself.

This self (Atman) is to be obtained through truth,
penance, right knowledge,
and constant practice of celibacy (self-control).
Within the body, the soul is a flame,
pure and luminous.

—Chandogya Upanishad, Chapter 8, Verse 3.3

This verse emphasizes the disciplined path to realizing the Atman (Self). The verse teaches that self-realization is not an intellectual exercise but a holistic process requiring a life of truth, penance, right knowledge, and self-control (brahmacharya).

These are seen as pillars that purify the mind and body, enabling one to perceive the eternal light of the soul within, described metaphorically as a luminous flame inside the body.

The flame symbolizes the pure consciousness that illuminates life. Just as a physical flame requires constant fuel and protection from the wind, the inner flame of the soul requires fuel in the form of disciplined living and truthfulness.

For instance, a person striving for self-realization may practice meditation (penance), seek wisdom (right knowledge), and maintain self-restraint in desires and actions (*brahmacharya*). Through these efforts, they gradually transcend the material world, gaining a deeper understanding of their eternal nature, the Atman.

Thank you for joining me on this journey.

I hope this book has inspired you to embrace the transformative power of 'no' and to live a more intentional and empowered life.